Sebastian Schaal

# Algorithmic Detection of Home Appliances from Smart Meter Data

Sebastian Schaal

# Algorithmic Detection of Home Appliances from Smart Meter Data

## Proof-of-concept implementation of Energy Disaggregation algorithms based on data generated from smart meters

Natural Sciences Series

**Impressum / Imprint**

Bibliografische Information der Deutschen Nationalbibliothek: Die Deutsche Nationalbibliothek verzeichnet diese Publikation in der Deutschen Nationalbibliografie; detaillierte bibliografische Daten sind im Internet über http://dnb.d-nb.de abrufbar.

Alle in diesem Buch genannten Marken und Produktnamen unterliegen warenzeichen-, marken- oder patentrechtlichem Schutz bzw. sind Warenzeichen oder eingetragene Warenzeichen der jeweiligen Inhaber. Die Wiedergabe von Marken, Produktnamen, Gebrauchsnamen, Handelsnamen, Warenbezeichnungen u.s.w. in diesem Werk berechtigt auch ohne besondere Kennzeichnung nicht zu der Annahme, dass solche Namen im Sinne der Warenzeichen- und Markenschutzgesetzgebung als frei zu betrachten wären und daher von jedermann benutzt werden dürften.

Bibliographic information published by the Deutsche Nationalbibliothek: The Deutsche Nationalbibliothek lists this publication in the Deutsche Nationalbibliografie; detailed bibliographic data are available in the Internet at http://dnb.d-nb.de.

Any brand names and product names mentioned in this book are subject to trademark, brand or patent protection and are trademarks or registered trademarks of their respective holders. The use of brand names, product names, common names, trade names, product descriptions etc. even without a particular marking in this work is in no way to be construed to mean that such names may be regarded as unrestricted in respect of trademark and brand protection legislation and could thus be used by anyone.

Coverbild / Cover image: www.ingimage.com

Verlag / Publisher:
AV Akademikerverlag
ist ein Imprint der / is a trademark of
OmniScriptum GmbH & Co. KG
Heinrich-Böcking-Str. 6-8, 66121 Saarbrücken, Deutschland / Germany
Email: info@akademikerverlag.de

Herstellung: siehe letzte Seite /
Printed at: see last page
**ISBN: 978-3-639-85846-4**

Copyright © 2015 OmniScriptum GmbH & Co. KG
Alle Rechte vorbehalten. / All rights reserved. Saarbrücken 2015

# Abstract

Studies show that the energy consumption of people can be reduced by providing them with consumption data of their appliances on a device level. As a means to measure only the aggregated load of a household and gaining insight into the device with post processing, the research field of non-intrusive appliance load monitoring (NALM) was defined. The generation of this type of data becomes easier with the introduction of digital energy meters. Smart meters provide an easy solution to extract momentary values of the energy consumption of the overall household which can be stored to be further processed. In this thesis, a new smart meter following the standards of Germany for a future roll-out is used to extract the overall data of the test household. Thereby, the procedure introduced can likely be reproduced at different sites in the future. Furthermore, three algorithmic approaches are presented to each detect one of the following major appliances: a freezer, a dryer, and a dishwasher. The characteristics of these devices were analyzed to extract the necessary parameter for the program. The algorithms rely on the detection of steps in real and reactive power, each coupled with one of the following features: cycle length detection (freezer), event duration consideration (dishwasher), and runtime pattern analysis (dryer). The implementation and test of the algorithms showed a 100% detection rate and only little deviations within the actual start and end time of the event. By using different parameters, this promising approach can likely be used for other appliances. All in all, this thesis works as a proof of concept, how NALM can successfully be implemented with little effort using a data granularity provided by smart meters.

# Table of Contents

# List of Abbreviations

| | |
|---|---|
| AOI | Appliance of interest |
| AP | Automatic Program |
| AS | Automatic-Setup |
| BSI | German Federal Office for Information Security (Bundesamt für Sicherheit in der Informationstechnik) |
| CRC | Cyclical Redundancy Check |
| EEP | Energy Efficiency Program |
| EnWG | German Energy Industry Act (Energiewirtschaftsgesetz) |
| FSM | Finite State Machine |
| IEC | International Electrotechnical Commission |
| LSB | Least Significant Bit |
| MID | European Measuring Instruments Directive |
| MS | Manual-Setup |
| NALM | Non-Intrusive Appliance Load Monitoring |
| PDU | Protocol Data Unit |
| RTU | Remote Terminal Unit |
| REDD | Reference Energy Disaggregation Data |
| TCP | Transmission Control Protocol |
| VDE | Association for Electrical, Electronic & Information Technologies (Verband der Elektrotechnik, Elektronik und Informationstechnik) |

# 1.    New Challenges for the Energy Supply of the Future

With the beginning of the 21st century, mankind is becoming increasingly aware of the new challenges of this era. The object of growth at any price is shifting towards the idea of ecological sustainability and the awareness of dwindling resources is a pressing issue in many cases. In order to tackle the future shortage of resources, stopping unnecessary waste and identifying saving potential is key. Especially the energy sector reveals a lot of starting points on an overall perspective as well as on a personal level.

## 1.1    Background

### 1.1.1    Energy Saving Efforts

Rising demand of energy in western countries as well as in developing countries is the driver for the dramatic increase of $CO_2$ emissions. Besides the general idea of increasing efficiency and reducing the consumption, the introduction of renewables was the mean for a greener energy approach. Different associations with different reach introduced plans for the future with goals on how much emissions and energy consumption should be reduced as well as the extend of integration of renewables. Having taken on some of the most ambitious plans, the European Union is the driving force. The second period of the Kyoto-protocol mainly includes obligations for countries in the EU to reduce greenhouse gases[1]. In October 2014, the EU committed to their climate policy framework, which includes a minimum 40 % reduction of greenhouse gas emissions compared to 1990 and at least a 27 % share of energy from renewables until 2030[2].

With the increase of renewables in the private and industrial sector, the energy production faces two important challenges. First, the energy production especially of solar cells is highly dependent on the time of the day, since it obviously correlates to the intensity of the sun. Therefore, the shift from e.g. nuclear power plants with a continuous production to renewables created an unsteadiness on the supply side. Furthermore, the generated energy of these renewables, especially photovoltaics in households, can be estimated over a period of time but hardly predicted for every situation in real-time. And second, there is an increasing fluctuation of energy consumption from the consumer as the demand side. Consequently, the stability of the energy grid is a critical challenge of today. The ability to plan consumption in more detail would enable a smart utilization of energy. A solution would be the change from the current way of supplying energy when it is needed to a sophisticated approach of consuming energy when it is supplied.

The major research field tackling this problem is the idea of smart grid. Making our grid smart can solve the problem of upcoming instabilities due to decentralized energy generation of renewables. Getting a real-time feedback on the actual consumption and generation of energy of every household would allow the energy supplier to secure a stable energy supply, avoid mismatches in energy supply and demand, and thereby increase efficiency. Nevertheless, the actual process of switching appliances on and off is still in the power of the customer. As an incentive for people to help align supply and demand, different pricing models can be offered. But using high-consuming devices such as a washing machine

---

[1] Frankfurter Allgemeine Zeitung, „Mini Kompromiss beim Welt-Klimagipfel", http://www.faz.net/aktuell/wirtschaft/kyoto-protokoll-verlaengert-mini-kompromiss-beim-welt-klimagipfel-11986836.html, retrieved Nov 11, 2014
[2] European Council, "Agreement on climate policy framework up to 2030", http://www.bundesregierung.de/Content/EN/Reiseberichte/2014/2014-10-22-europaeischer-rat-oktober.html, Nov 16, 2014

in times of excess supply can only be rewarded, if there is a way to track these actions. Obviously, this is an area, where normal metering installations in our homes reach their limits.

## 1.1.2 Motivation of Disaggregated Data

For the purposes mentioned above, the introduction of smart meters has been discussed over a period of time. The details about the digital version of the current energy meter and political implications in Germany will be outlined in Chapter 2. Besides the advantages for the energy supplier mentioned in the previous chapter and the automation of the meter readings, there is a lot of potential benefit for the inhabitant of a household. In times of rising energy prices, reducing the own consumption is one major issue. This, however, requires a lot of effort and countless checks on the analog meters to create only a little transparency about the energy usage in private households.

Research has shown that providing feedback about the current consumption to the inhabitant reduces the energy bill through increased awareness [5]. But often it is up to the user how to interpret a certain piece of data. The fact that there is live monitoring might already increase the general awareness, but the user has no definite insight into what is driving the demand at a certain point of time. The key to identifying patterns that result from bad habits and the truly high consuming devices in a household lies in monitoring on a device level. Only if the inhabitant is able to see e.g. how much the refrigerator consumes in comparison to the washing machine, can he or she act sensibly.

There are different ways to generate consumption data on a device level. The traditional approach would involve monitoring every appliance by its own and collecting the data at one place for display. A newer possibility for this purpose is the use of smart plugs which are intermediate plugs to the power outlet with a communication unit. However, equipping your whole house with these devices is expensive and inconvenient. Ideally, one could have just one central metering point to increase convenience and even leverage existing hardware to drive down costs.

The technique behind this approach is referred to as energy disaggregation, since it tries to find the origin that creates the aggregated overall load that is active in a household. This aggregated data could be measured by digital energy meters like upcoming smart meters. This way, an upcoming hardware can be leveraged to get the relevant data. The disaggregation itself is a complex problem and requires additional data processing. Hereby, the signature of appliances will be identified in the aggregated load curve to identify their presence. However, the challenge is to transform the data in a way that makes a clear separation of appliances possible.

## 1.1.3 Existing Techniques

The process of detecting the presence of an appliance within the overall load curve relies on a cluster analysis. Since every appliance is not deterministic but influenced by external factors, the behavior can never be predicted in its entirety. Therefore, even a characteristic behavior varies over time, which motivates the approach of clustering similar data and referring it to a certain appliance or component of a device. The challenge hereby is to find a dimension, where the clustering process can be done exclusively to ensure a clear assignment. The efficiency of this process mostly relies on a few characteristics of the data delivered by the measurement equipment as well as the algorithm used for the appliance detection. For the data, its granularity and the availability of different measurement units are relevant. For the algorithm the most important differentiation is between the usage of prior knowledge of the single appliances to detect their signature and a fully automated process, which learns the characteristics of appliances during runtime.

Historically, the idea of disaggregating energy data to detect individual consumers goes back to the late 1980s. At that time, measuring the consumption of single appliances with metering devices directly at their point of power supply was common practice in order to monitor them. The means of placing sensors on individual appliances is considered intrusive, since it acts as an intrusion onto the property of the consumer. In contrast to this approach, George Hart opened up the research field of Non-Intrusive Appliance Load Monitoring (NALM, also NIALM, NILM, or NIALMS) which is discussed in more detail in Chapter 2. His algorithm uses real and reactive power within data sets with granularities of approximately 1 Hz (one measurement per second). Hart assumes that most appliances change their current state by showing a step-like change in their power consumption. To quantify these transitions he uses the deltas of the real and reactive power for his analysis. He constructs an "action house", where the changes in real and reactive power are plotted against each other. This constitutes the dimension where he performs his clustering to identify single appliances. He generally defines three kinds of appliances: on/off switching devices, Finite State Machines (FSM), and those with an unpredictable profile [4].

Over the years there has been a lot of research on this topic, but the core of Hart's approach is still valid. From today's perspective, not only the possibility of performing NALM, but the feasibility is important. To make this concept attractive to a large group of people, the hardware should be available and affordable for everyone. With the roll-out of smart meters planned in many countries as outlined above, it is sensible to develop methods that leverage the created data. Therefore, this thesis tries to create NALM algorithms, which are capable of performing based on data generated by smart meters.

Ever since the topic of NALM existed, there have been concerns about data privacy. A sophisticated analysis of aggregated smart meter data could enable insight into the habits of the inhabitants of a household. This becomes even more efficient by using potential high-frequency sampling smart meters [6]. Even it is not officially declared to this point, the roll-out of devices with such a high granularity is not very likely, since they do not bring any benefits in the simple use case of transmitting average consumption reports to the energy suppliers [7].

Since current smart meter models enable the extraction of data with a granularity around 1 Hz through a local interface, the inhabitants can leverage this data to gain insight into their energy consumption. This data already enables the disaggregation of the major appliances, as shown within the study of Armel [6]. Therefore, choosing this approach is tempting, because it offers a solution for a potentially large amount of people.

## 1.2  Aim of the Thesis

This Bachelor thesis demonstrates how appliances in a normal household can be detected by using data gained from one measurement point where aggregated data is available. The data is generated through a smart meter which will follow the German standard for future energy meters. The interface used for the generation of data is the industry conform RS-485 port combined with the Modbus RTU protocol.

The thesis provides insight into the generation of data with this protocol and the necessary scripts to process the data. Algorithms to detect the current state of home appliances are tested on the generated data set. A freezer, a dishwasher, and a dryer are used as sample appliances. With prior knowledge of the load curves of these devices, parameters extracted from this data serve as input for the algorithms to detect the appliances. Within this thesis, three algorithmic approaches are shown and tested according to their accuracy and reliability.

*The aim of the thesis is the programming of algorithms which can detect when a certain appliance in the test household is used. Through the measurements on single appliances, prior knowledge about the load curve exists and is used to extract input parameters for the algorithms. As it reveals potential for a later use case, the use of hardware and software to generate data from smart meters should be explored.*

## 1.3    Research Direction and Methodology

In a first step, the author created a database for the further research work in a three person test household. On the one hand, he extracted the overall consumption data of the household from an installed digital smart meter. On the other hand, he used a power meter to measure the load curves of the three appliances of interest (AOIs) as references. The author's research focused on the fields of NALM, energy disaggregation, and pattern recognition. The analysis of literature on the detection of appliances with a central measurement unit revealed different options for device detection. The author tested some methods on the test data to reveal their potential for the specific use case. In addition to literature research, he contacted experts via e-mail and telephone to give their input on the most sensible hardware and approaches to use.

An analysis of the data and former approaches of device detection revealed the most promising directions to be followed. Consequently, the author implemented three different algorithm approaches in Matlab to perform the task. By applying the programs on the data set, the research question, if and how reliably home appliances can be detected, should be answered. The author defined assessment criteria to evaluate the algorithms and compare the different approaches.

## 1.4    Delimitation of the Thesis

As described in a prior section, the research area, where information about individual devices is gained from a central measurement unit, was introduced in the 1980s by George Hart. The paragraph showed the variety of research approaches and the different quality of data.

This thesis combines the well-known idea of detecting steps in the real and reactive power with new approaches, targeting specific appliances classes. It introduces an optimization in detection of appliances with a power cycle, an easy to parameterize load curve, or a runtime pattern. Thereby, a very reliable and accurate method is created. In addition, the thesis works on data generated from the latest smart meter technology. It is very likely that the granularity of data used in this thesis will become a standard for smart meters in the future. Consequently, the techniques created in this thesis could become relevant and useable with future smart meters. In addition, the thesis provides a way to extract and interpret data via the industry protocol Modbus RTU without professional software.

## 1.5    Outline of the Thesis

The thesis contains six chapters. The introduction motivates the relevance of the thesis and delivers some general information on it. In Chapter 2, the terms smart meter and NALM are explained in greater detail. Chapter 3 outlines the measurement and logging equipment setup as well as the usage of the required software. In Chapter 4, the data of the three AOIs and the overall household are discussed. Chapter 5 describes the assessment criteria of the algorithms, their implementation, and their success. The last chapter discusses the limitations of the thesis and the future work to be done.

# 2. Definitions and Terminology

## 2.1 Smart Meter

A smart meter is the intelligent version of the general Ferraris electricity meter which is currently installed in 43 million German households [8]. It is able to perform detailed measurement of several quantities and transmit data via an interface. If the potential of this interface is leveraged and a communication module is added, the smart meter is able to transmit relevant consumption data to the energy supplier for billing purposes. A the Climate Group defines it as: "Advanced meters that identify consumption in more detail than conventional meters and communicate via a network back to the utility for monitoring and billing purposes" [9].

Obviously, this raises privacy concerns. On the one hand, the energy suppliers could get a relatively detailed insight into the habits of their customers, depending on the granularity of the data transmitted. On the other hand, if the transmission of data was not totally secure, cyber criminals would be able to extract the data and use it for criminal activities. If data of several households is stolen, a network of houses could be monitored simultaneously. Furthermore, algorithms could detect homes which are not inhabited at the moment and reveal these properties as potential targets. Therefore, an expert committee in Germany spent a great deal of effort on securing the transmission and interface structure.[10]

This new approach differentiates between a certified smart meter and currently available digital meters which can be installed behind the official Ferraris energy meter. In a way, the current digital meter is part of the system which will become the standard in German households. In addition to the digital measurement unit the future infrastructure will also contain a smart meter gateway which is responsible for transmitting only relevant data to the energy supplier. This division enables the smart meter to measure several quantities which could be of interest to the inhabitant, without making them directly accessible to the energy supplier over a communication module. A current solution is the Smart Meter Gateway of Dr. Neuhaus which is qualified for roll-out.[3] Fig. 1 shows the different system components required to perform the automated smart metering.

A paradox in the German history of smart meters is the fact that they should have already been heavily installed. Following the directive 2010/31/EU by the European Union of 2010 the German government integrated a paragraph about the installation of measurement systems into the German Energy Act (EnWG). Paragraph 21 clearly stated that an installation would be obligatory if the process was technically and economically feasible [11]. Since there were many things still unclear and reports coming up, stating that these systems are neither secure nor helping to save money, the grey area in the paragraph was used as a loophole to avoid the installation of smart meters. However, the new plans of the German Federal Office for Information Security (BSI) and the Association for Electrical, Electronic & Information Technologies (VDE) seem to be able to overcome the doubts, set a future standard, and enable the Germany-wide roll-out. Serious efforts are done to enable the roll-out in 2020 within the "Messsysteme 2020" campaign of the VDE [12].

---

[3] Dr. Neuhaus, SMARTY IQ-GPRS, http://www.neuhaus.de/Produkte/Smart_Metering/SMARTY_IQ-GPRS.php, retrieved Jan 14, 2015

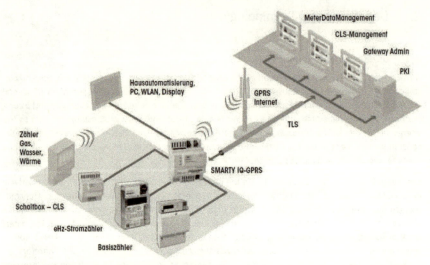

Fig. 1: Structure of a smart meter gateway system by Dr. Neuhaus
Source: http://www.neuhaus.de/Produkte/Smart_Metering/SMARTY_IQ-GPRS.php

A standard smart meter is generally able to measure the real, reactive, and apparent power, voltage, current, frequency, and additional figures which can be computed from the mentioned quantities. Since the supply of energy in Germany is performed over three-phase current, all these measurements are available for each of the different phases. As already outlined in the introduction, it is not likely that energy suppliers will use high-frequency sampling hardware in the future because there are no real benefits without intruding into the privacy of the consumer. Consequently, this thesis uses a 1 Hz granularity to generate the necessary data as outlined in Chapter 3.

## 2.2 Non-Intrusive Appliance Load Monitoring

Measuring the consumption of single appliances with metering devices at the appliances' power supply directly was common practice to monitor the device. This means of placing sensors on individual appliances is considered intrusive, since it acts as an intrusion onto the property of the consumer [4]. In contrast to this approach, George Hart opened up the research field of Nonintrusive Appliance Load Monitoring, abbreviated NALM (also NIALM, NILM, or NIALMS). His publications [4, 13, 14] introduce a system which is capable of detecting the runtime of a device by identifying the switch-on and switch-off time. He differentiates between three kinds of devices: two-state devices with just an on- and off-state, Finite State Machines (FSM) with deterministic transitions of states, and devices with an unpredictable profile. His algorithm works for the first two types of devices, since it is based on step changes in the real and reactive power. Assuming that the steps of a device in its power consumption happen nearly instantaneously one can further predict that no two devices switch states at the same time. Therefore, steps in the overall load curve can be linked to a switching process of a certain appliance. Fig. 2 of Hart's publication [4] indicates those processes on the basis of just the real power.

This delivers a good first approach, but fails on differentiating between appliances with the same real power consumption. To add another dimension, the reactive power was introduced as a second type of data. Since the steps in the two types of power seem to be characteristic, they were calculated and plotted in a p-diagram, which illustrates the deltas of real and reactive power in dependence of each other. Fig. 3 shows a clustering of certain appliances according to their signature space. It is already visible that devices with relatively small power consumption are more difficult to differentiate.

In his work Hart divides NALM into a Manual-Setup (MS) and an Automatic-Setup (AS) version. The MS-NALM has prior knowledge of the devices' signatures due to intrusively gained profiles or switching

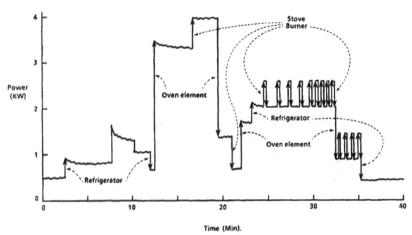

Fig. 2: Graphic of Hart's publication showing step changes due to individual events
Source: [4]

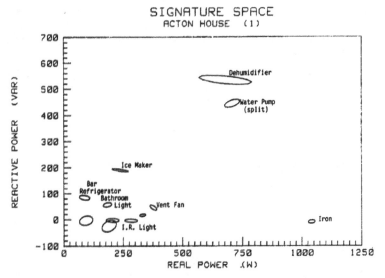

Fig. 3: P-Diagram of Hart's publication (1992) showing signature spaces of certain appliances
Source: [4]

off all other devices manually to measure the relevant data. AS-NALM is supposed to run fully automatically while learning about the apparent devices from a priori knowledge of possible characteristics.

In addition, the system described is considered as off-line, since it performs a kind of post processing of past events. On-line would be able to deliver instant feedback to the user.

The original NALM algorithm follows these four core steps:

1. "Edge Detection" identifies the size and time of step changes
2. "Cluster Analysis" groups a cluster of similar changes in a p-diagram
3. "Build Appliance Models" combines cluster to match a two-state and afterwards FSM appliance
4. "Track Behavior" signs events to appliances, tries to solve irregularities, and assigns the remaining clusters with a best likelihood principle.

In 1999, Drenker and Kader described the success of Hart's system which was developed as a prototype [15]. It was performing very well for On/Off and FSM appliances but failed for others. Christopher Laughman and his co-authors mention that there are three main problems of Hart's approach which (according to them) result from his assumptions [16]. First, Hart assumes a clearness in the signature clusters which is problematic for larger households, since there are potential overlaps (e.g. heaters and motors are part of several devices and all show similar characteristics). Second, he implies that stationary states can only change through steps. This is in some ways true for simple devices such as a refrigerator, but more complex appliances like e.g. a washing machine are not as easy to detect. Third, the analysis can only be performed off-line, which means that it is a post-processing technique without the ability of delivering instant feedback. Especially problem one and two can be solved by using data of higher granularity. In his publication, Laughman used a sampling frequency of 8 kHz [16].

In Europe it was Sultanem who started research on NALM systems with three-phase current in 1991. In contrast to Hart's setting, he was measuring data at a higher sampling frequency of 1.5 kHz, which enables a view on the oscillation behavior and helps to identify the single appliances. He also uses differential quantities of real and reactive power to identify state changes in devices. The workflow is as follows: first, learning of load characteristics is applied, second, the acquisition of events is performed and third, the loads are identified. Again, this method shows weaknesses for devices with a continuously changing power demand [17].

In 1994, Roos et al. proposed another method of NALM which was designed for industry loads and works with a variety of neural networks to identify the devices. In addition to the known values of real and reactive power, Roos added a third dimension called the harmonic distortion. This distortion appears in modern, semiconductor-controlled devices, since they incorporate a current draw which does not strictly follow a sinusoidal waveform. This measurement requires a high sampling rate similar to those in the work of Sultanem and Laughman [18].

After this pioneer work there was little development in the consecutive years. One reason for that lies in the expensive and impractical setup which is required to attain experimental data. This need was served by Kolter et al. in 2011 by providing the Reference Energy Disaggregation Data Set (REDD) [19]. As probably the largest data set available it contains high resolution data of a number of houses with a frequency of 15 kHz as well as data of individual circuits in the home at 0.5 Hz and plug-level monitors of appliances at 1 Hz. To this day, many publications use the REDD as a basis for the algorithmic development. However, the data is generated in homes in the United States and therefore implies a two-phase current instead of the three-phase current used in Germany. A similar dataset was delivered by Anderson et al. in 2012. In addition to a high sampling frequency of 12 kHz for the entire house they used plug-level monitors with up to 1 kHz. Moreover, Anderson focused on collecting data on so-called events of each appliance to support the development of event-based algorithms [20].

Beyond these sampling rates, Froehlich et al. showed disaggregation techniques relying on frequencies up to hundreds of Kilohertz [7]. Some appliances produce unique electrical noise during the continuous on-state or by being turned on and off. This phenomenon can be used to identify devices and is especially suitable for computers or TVs. However, as outlined above, since the usage of smart meters as a measurement unit is the focus of this thesis, high frequencies will not be considered in the following.

# 3. Measurement and Logging Equipment Setup

This chapter focuses on the measurement and logging equipment which was used to gain the necessary data for the analysis. Details about the exact products and setup are given to ensure reproducibility. Generally, the installation of two systems was required. The first task of measuring the aggregated power consumption was performed by a smart meter which follows the latest directives. In addition, a power meter was needed which is able to measure several quantities at once and transmit them over an interface to ensure the data logging.

## 3.1 Smart Meter

The smart meter which was used for the setup of this thesis was a product of the Berg GmbH in Martinsried. The version B23-312 is a three-phase electronic meter with accuracy class 1 approved by the European Measuring Instruments Directive (MID) and the International Electrotechnical Commission (IEC). It supports direct current measurements up to 65A and communicates over the RS-485 interface with Modbus RTU protocol which will be discussed below. The meter measures the quantities real, reactive, and apparent power, current, voltage, phase angles, and power factor for all these phases. The values are stored in internal registers and have to be requested sending Modbus commands. The mentioned accuracy can be guaranteed within a voltage range of 20 % around the nominal voltage and a current range of 5% around the base current.

### 3.1.1 Setup and Details

The Berg meter can be installed in different ways. First, it can be transformed or directly connected and second, a two, three, or four wire connection can be used. Due to the simplicity of setting up the meter, the three wire directly connected setup was used first. Unfortunately, this setup disabled some possible measurements involving the potential of the neutral conductor, which will be shown in more detail in the next section. To solve this issue, the neutral conductor was installed to enable the generation of a larger variety of data. Fig. 4 shows the connecting diagram of the Berg meter in the described setup [1].

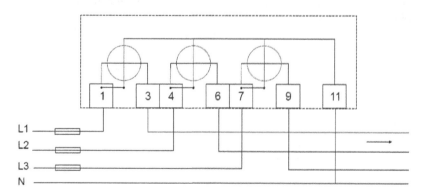

*Fig. 4: Connecting diagram of Berg meter in described setup*
Source: [1]

## 3.1.2   Interface and Protocol

The Berg meter contains a RS-485 serial port which can be used for the communication with the meter over the Modbus Remote Terminal Unit (RTU) protocol.

The Modbus protocol is a communication protocol which was developed by Modicon in 1979. It is based on a Master/Slave or Client/Server architecture and became the de-facto standard in the industry. The open protocol defines the message structure and thereby how the master can send a request to the slave and how the response is structured. There are different versions of how to connect a slave device with the Master and three different operating modes. Via a serial port or Ethernet the data is transmitted in Modbus ASCII, RTU, or Transmission Control Protocol (TCP) [21]. Within the setup of this thesis, the Berg meter uses Modbus RTU and is connected over a RS-485 serial port which will be described in more detail in the next chapter.

The RTU Transmission Mode uses an 8-bit binary coding system, where each byte contains two 4-bit hexadecimal characters [21]. Each message has to be transmitted in a continuous stream of 11-bit characters which involve:

**The format (11 bits) for each character in RTU mode is:** [21]

Bits per character:    1 start bit    8 data bits (LSB sent first)    0 or 1 bit for parity    1 or 2 stop bit(s)

For the parity, "even" is the default one, however, "odd" and "no parity" can also be used. In case of "none" as parity, a second stop bit is sent instead of the parity. Most importantly, the settings of the logging equipment and the software have to match each other.

The bytes are grouped in a RTU message frame, which has a clear structure shown in Fig. 5. The inner part is called Modbus Protocol Data Unit (Modbus PDU), which is independent from the underlying communication layer and contains the information for the task to be performed in the device. Adding an address byte for clear referencing and an error checking byte delivers the Modbus Serial Line PDU as the whole frame. Each frame is separated by a silent period of minimum 3.5 characters and the sequences within the frame are separated by a maximum of 1.5 characters of silence. If the timeout between two characters is bigger than that, the whole frame is considered incorrect. Higher baud rates make this strict separation a lot harder, which is why baud rates higher than 19,200 Bps are assigned fixed values. The variations are shown in Table 1.

*Table 1: Used baud rates and corresponding time intervals of silent periods*

| Baud rate | Time for 3.5 characters | Time for 1.5 characters |
|-----------|------------------------|------------------------|
| 1,200 | 32.083 ms | 13.750 ms |
| 2,400 | 16.042 ms | 6.875 ms |
| 4,800 | 8.021 ms | 3.437 ms |
| 9,600 | 4.010 ms | 1.719 ms |
| 19,200 | 2.005 ms | 0.859 ms |
| 38,400 | 1.750 ms | 0.750 ms |
| 57,600 | 1.750 ms | 0.750 ms |
| 115,200 | 1.750 ms | 0.750 ms |

Source: Own illustration

The different parts of the frame serve specific purposes. In the following, the structure for reading holding-registers is outlined in more detail.

**Address:**     Since Modbus is a master/slave communication protocol, the master has to indicate which of the possible 247 slaves it is referring to. The allowed address byte ranges from 0x01 (1) to 0xF7 (247), whereas 0x00 (0) is the broadcast address and 0xF8 (248) to 0xFF (255) are reserved.

**Function:**     The function code indicates the operation which the code is performing. For the Berg meter only three codes are supported. Reading of holding-registers is done with 0x03 (3), writing to single registers with 0x06 (6), and writing to multiple registers with 0x10 (16).

**Data:**     The data part is the only thing that differs from a request to a response. For a request, the bytes contain the start address of the registers and the number of consecutive registers which should be transmitted. If one wants to reach just single parts of the registers, more than one request is needed. The first byte of the response indicates the number of relevant bytes, which will follow. Since the registers of the Berg meter have 16 bits, two bytes are needed per register. As the data part of the response cannot be longer than 252 bytes and the byte count is obligatory, a maximum of 125 consecutive registers with 250 bytes can be reached with one request.

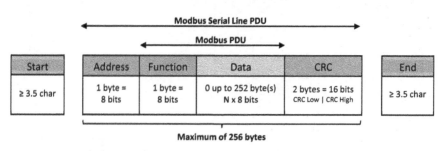

Fig. 5: Schematic of a frame in the Modbus RTU protocol for reading a holding register
Source: Own illustration, [1]

**CRC:**     The Cyclical Redundancy Check (CRC) fields deliver a control value to identify transmission errors. It is built by the transmitting devices from the rest of the bytes of the message and then appended. The receiving device extracts the transmitted CRC value and then builds its own CRC from the rest of the received message. If the two values match, the device expects a successful transmission. For the generation of the CRC the polynomial 0xA001 is used while the initial register is pre-loaded with 0xFFFF. The details about the procedure can be found in the appendix.

The two generated bytes of the CRC are appended in reverse order, so that the low byte is transmitted before the high byte. This was defined in the Modbus standard and is not correctly outlined in the manual of the Berg meter [1, 21].

To identify the registers and their corresponding values, the Berg manual delivered a detailed table. For the purposes of the thesis, only the momentary values were of interest.

Table 2 shows the detailed view on the momentary values and the mapping to the registers. As already stated in the previous chapter, the setup with three wires does not allow the measurement of all quantities. The green shadowed rows indicate the possible measurement with the three wire installation, the red ones are only possible with the neutral conductor [1].

*Table 2: Mapping of registers to their values*

| # | Quantity | Details | Start Reg. (Hex) | Size | Res. | Unit | Value range | Data type |
|---|----------|---------|------------------|------|------|------|-------------|-----------|
| 1 | Voltage | L1-N | 23296 (0x5B00) | 2 | 01 | V | | Unsigned |
| 2 | Voltage | L2-N | 23298 (0x 5B02) | 2 | 01 | V | | Unsigned |
| 3 | Voltage | L3-N | 23300 (0x 5B04) | 2 | 01 | V | | Unsigned |
| 4 | Voltage | L1-L2 | 23302 (0x 5B06) | 2 | 01 | V | | Unsigned |
| 5 | Voltage | L3-L2 | 23304 (0x 5B08) | 2 | 01 | V | | Unsigned |
| 6 | Voltage | L1-L3 | 23306 (0x 5B0A) | 2 | 01 | V | | Unsigned |
| 7 | Current | L1 | 23308 (0x 5B0C) | 2 | 001 | A | | Unsigned |
| 8 | Current | L2 | 23310 (0x 5B0E) | 2 | 001 | A | | Unsigned |
| 9 | Current | L3 | 23312 (0x 5B10) | 2 | 001 | A | | Unsigned |
| 10 | Current | N | 23314 (0x 5B12) | 2 | 001 | A | | Unsigned |
| 11 | Active power | Total | 23316 (0x 5B14) | 2 | 001 | W | | Signed |
| 12 | Active power | L1 | 23318 (0x 5B16) | 2 | 001 | W | | Signed |
| 13 | Active power | L2 | 23320 (0x 5B18) | 2 | 001 | W | | Signed |
| 14 | Active power | L3 | 23322 (0x 5B1A) | 2 | 001 | W | | Signed |
| 15 | Reactive power | Total | 23324 (0x 5B1C) | 2 | 001 | var | | Signed |
| 16 | Reactive power | L1 | 23326 (0x 5B1E) | 2 | 001 | var | | Signed |
| 17 | Reactive power | L2 | 23328 (0x 5B20) | 2 | 001 | var | | Signed |
| 18 | Reactive power | L3 | 23330 (0x 5B22) | 2 | 001 | var | | Signed |
| 19 | Apparent power | Total | 23332 (0x 5B24) | 2 | 001 | VA | | Signed |
| 20 | Apparent power | L1 | 23334 (0x 5B26) | 2 | 001 | VA | | Signed |
| 21 | Apparent power | L2 | 23336 (0x 5B28) | 2 | 001 | VA | | Signed |
| 22 | Apparent power | L3 | 23338 (0x 5B2A) | 2 | 001 | VA | | Signed |
| 23 | Frequency | | 23340 (0x 5B2C) | 1 | 001 | Hz | | Unsigned |
| 24 | Phase angle power | Total | 23341 (0x 5B2D) | 1 | 01 | ° | -180° – +180° | Signed |
| 25 | Phase angle power | L1 | 23342 (0x 5B2E) | 1 | 01 | ° | -180° – +180° | Signed |
| 26 | Phase angle power | L2 | 23343 (0x 5B2F) | 1 | 01 | ° | -180° – +180° | Signed |
| 27 | Phase angle power | L3 | 23344 (0x 5B30) | 1 | 01 | ° | -180° – +180° | Signed |
| 28 | Phase angle voltage | L1 | 23345 (0x 5B31) | 1 | 01 | ° | -180° – +180° | Signed |
| 29 | Phase angle voltage | L2 | 23346 (0x 5B32) | 1 | 01 | ° | -180° – +180° | Signed |
| 30 | Phase angle voltage | L3 | 23347 (0x 5B33) | 1 | 01 | ° | -180° – +180° | Signed |
| | Unused | - | 23348 (0x 5B34) | 3 | - | - | - | - |
| 31 | Phase angle current | L1 | 23351 (0x 5B37) | 1 | 01 | - | -180° – +180° | Signed |
| 32 | Phase angle current | L2 | 23352 (0x 5B38) | 1 | 01 | - | -180° – +180° | Signed |
| 34 | Phase angle current | L3 | 23353 (0x 5B39) | 1 | 01 | - | -180° – +180° | Signed |
| 35 | Power factor | Total | 23354 (0x 5B3A) | 1 | 0001 | - | -1.000 – +1.000 | Signed |
| 36 | Power factor | L1 | 23355 (0x 5B3B) | 1 | 0001 | - | -1.000 – +1.000 | Signed |
| 37 | Power factor | L2 | 23356 (0x 5B3C) | 1 | 0001 | - | -1.000 – +1.000 | Signed |
| 38 | Power factor | L3 | 23357 (0x 5B3D) | 1 | 0001 | - | -1.000 – +1.000 | Signed |
| 39 | Current quadrant | Total | 23358 (0x 5B3E) | 1 | 1 | - | 1 – 4 | Unsigned |

| 40 | Current quadrant | L1 | 23359 (0x 5B3F) | 1 | 1 | - | 1 – 4 | Unsigned |
| 41 | Current quadrant | L2 | 23360 (0x 5B40) | 1 | 1 | - | 1 – 4 | Unsigned |
| 42 | Current quadrant | L3 | 23361 (0x 5B41) | 1 | 1 | - | 1 – 4 | Unsigned |

Source: Own illustration, [1]

### 3.1.3 Data Logging

The data logging was performed with the described interface over the Modbus protocol. To leverage the measurement data of the smart meter, data had to be extracted by sending continuous requests and logging the responses.

As already outlined, the Berg meter was ordered in the version containing a RS-485 communication port. This interface was connected with an RS-485 to USB converter from Digitus which will be referred to as the Digitus converter in the following. The RS-485 is a half-duplex interface that uses an inverted and non-inverted channel to transmit the signal. The potential difference between the two conductors indicate whether a high or low signal was sent. However, different manufacturers use different conventions to indicate the inverted and non-inverted pin at their devices.

Fig. 7: Picture of Digitus converter (left) and Berg meter (right)
Source: [2] / [1]

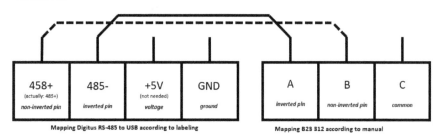

Fig. 6: Connecting diagram of Digitus converter (left) to Berg meter (right)
Source: Own illustration

The Digitus converter made it relatively simple, since it used a plus and minus convention. The 458+ (which is supposed to be 485+) corresponds to the non-inverted pin and the 485- corresponds to the inverted pin [2]. For the Berg meter, another convention with A, B, and C was used. The problem hereby is that most manufacturers follow the non-standard declaration and make A the non-inverted and B the inverted pin. However, the Berg meter follows the convention used in the RS-485 standard, which indicates A as the inverted and B as the non-inverted pin [22]. The mapping of the single components and the connection diagram can be found in Fig. 6.

After installing the hardware, some settings of the Berg meter have to be applied and tracked to align the setup with the logging software later on. First, the protocol had to be set to Modbus and for the address of the slave "1" was chosen, since there is no other slave on the bus. Second, 19200 was applied for the baud rate, which corresponds to 5.73 ms per character. This is a standard value and sufficient for the desired granularity of one value every second (it allows about 1745 characters). Third, "none" was selected for the parity.

The next task involved sending cyclic requests to the slave and logging the responses. For this purpose, the software FieldTalk modpoll 3.4 was used, which is a command line based Modbus master simulator and test utility. It delivers a solution for different operating systems and the various Modbus protocol. For the setup of the thesis, the Windows version with the RTU protocol in a read-only manner was used. Fig. 8 illustrates the command and its meaning [3].

With this command, all the available momentary values can be extracted. By adding the windows pipe operator ">" and the name of a new .txt file, the data can be saved. From this raw format, the data is imported into Matlab for further data processing. To transform the raw data into a suitable format, the hexadecimal values of the registers are extracted, merged if two of them belong to a 32 bit representation, converted according to their signed or unsigned nature, and finally stored in a new table. From this stage, the data can be displayed in plots or processed in other desired ways.

After eliminating all the primary implementation problems on the hardware and software side, one critical issue stayed: the timing problem. With the modpoll tool it is only possible to advise the program to send out the next request at a certain time after receiving the response. Therefore, if one desires to receive one value package every second, one has to take the process time of the response into account. If a higher granularity is achieved, the surplus data can be eliminated in post processing. Analysis of prior test sequences delivered the insight that the processing time did not exceed 15 ms on a regular basis. Consequently, a waiting time of 985 ms was chosen as seen in Fig. 8. As already stated, the surplus data was then eliminated by estimating a constant offset in the extraction time. E.g. if 601 values were extracted in 3 minutes, the 301st value was deleted to minimize the time mismatch. Similarly, a reconstruction script was created in case of a longer average processing time. Since the timeout parameters were chosen wisely, this was only needed for former tests and not for the final test data set.

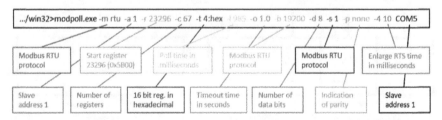

Fig. 8: Breakdown of command for FieldTalk modpoll tool
Source: Own illustration, [3]

## 3.2    Appliance Logger

In addition to the measurement of the aggregated data, another device was needed to extract the exact signatures of the AOIs. The challenge hereby was to find a logger which followed certain criteria:

-    It should have a possibility to be connected to an appliance via a power outlet
-    It should have an interface and internal storage to transmit and save the data
-    It should be capable of logging with all the maximum possible currents in a household being available
-    It should deliver a granularity of 1 Hz or 1 value every second

The simple and most convenient energy loggers on the market could not hold the last criterion. Although some of these devices were able to measure momentary values every second, the storage of this data was only possible in an accumulated manner every minute. Alternatively, multimeters with a power adapter and computer interface were possible candidates. However, they lacked the ability to log data for more than 20 seconds, if a current above 5 A was applied which was the case for almost the entire program cycle of the dryer and the dishwasher. Finally, there was a device from Christ-Elektronik GmbH which offered the functionality needed for the mentioned criteria.

### 3.2.1   Characteristics and Logging

The power measurement device CLM1000 Professional Plus is an easy to use meter with a power outlet connected to it. In addition, it contains a mini USB port to connect the device to a computer. On the different pages of its screen one can access all the momentary data. For logging purposes the CLM1000 contains two methods. On the one hand, the CLM1000 has an internal storage which is able to save data up to 24 hours in 1 second time intervals. On the other hand, the data logging can be performed instantaneously with a connected computer [23].

The software used for the logging purpose is called "hterm.exe". The general interface is shown in Fig. 9. Once the COM-port and the Modbus setting are applied, the data transmission can start. Especially for transmitting a 24 hours data block, 115,200 baud as the highest rate is selected. The data from the program can then be exported into a .csv file and further processed in Matlab.

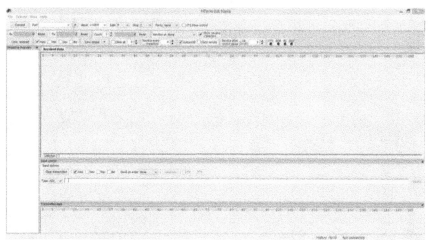

*Fig. 9: General interface of HTerm software*
Source: Own illustration (screenshot)

# 4. Analysis of Load Profiles

The following chapter delivers insight into the data that was generated with the measurement and logging system described in the previous chapter. In a first paragraph, the load curve of three important appliances found in many households will be illustrated. A dishwasher, a freezer, and a dryer serve as the AOIs for the following part of the thesis. They are analyzed on behalf of their characteristics, which are then quantified to serve as input data for a later stage. The second paragraph displays the aggregated data extracted from the Berg meter. Similar to the AOIs, the overall load curve is examined and its characteristics are identified. Furthermore, first estimations are made about how each of the three AOIs could possibly be recognized in the aggregated data.

## 4.1 Analysis of Individual Appliances

This paragraph will introduce the three AOIs, which were examined in greater detail. The measurements were taken with the appliance logger CLM1000, described in Chapter 3.

### 4.1.1 Dryer (Phase 3)

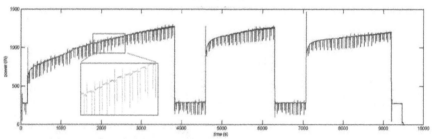

*Fig. 10: Sample load curve of dryer (bed sheets program)*
Source: Own illustration

Fig. 10 shows a sample drying cycle of the dryer in the test household. The appliance was produced by the firm AEG as the model Electrolux Öko-Lavatherm and it was connected to phase 3 of the household current. In this example, a standard bed sheets program was used. One important finding was that no two drying processes are perfectly unique. Obviously, a bed sheets program differs from one for sport clothes, but even the same program settings led to different curves, strongly depending on the amount and condition of the clothes. However, there are some characteristics which are similar throughout the different settings.

Between the spinning cycles, there are slots of around 13 minutes, where the standard power is 270 W. At the same power, there is a short initial slot before the cycles start. Every cycle shows overshooting due to the starting current of the electric motor of a few hundred watts. Within the cycles, the devices show a ramp-up in power. The first cycle starts at around 650 W, the following at 900 W, and they all end at approx. 1250 W, followed by a characteristic drop of 1000 W. The number of spinning cycles show no real correlation. There are events with only two or less cycles but also some with up to eight.

The most striking pattern of the dryer is its periodic drops in power that happen throughout the whole washing process, including the spinning and pause slots. The extract in the red box clearly shows the sequence, which is characteristic for the bed sheets program. Every program has these characteristic drops, but with a slightly different magnitude and in different intervals. While every program reveals

27

different intervals, only the jeans program significantly differs in the magnitude of the drops. The exact values can be seen in Table 5.

As this pattern is so clearly visible in the single device data, it can be assumed that it could be found in the aggregated data. In times when the dryer is active, these characteristic drops should happen significantly more often than in other times and ideally follow the examined pattern.

Table 3: Parameters of dryer event for bed sheets program

|  | Initial | First cycle | Pause | Following cycle | End |
|---|---|---|---|---|---|
| Power | 270 W <br> 30 var | 650 W to 1250 W <br> 250 var to 380 var | 270 W <br> 44 var | 900 W to 1250 W <br> 280 var to 380 var | 270 W <br> 48 var |
| Time | 3 min | varying | 13 min | varying | 4.5 min |

Every 20 s or 60 s drop around 60 to 200 W

Source: Own illustration

For the test period, the following events were detected:

Table 4: Dryer events during test period

| # | Start | End | Program |
|---|---|---|---|
| 1 | Dec 1, 2014 14:02 | Dec 1, 2014 16:50 | Bed sheets |
| 2 | Dec 1, 2014 17:40 | Dec 1, 2014 19:07 | Mix program |
| 3 | Dec 2, 2014 12:54 | Dec 2, 2014 15:44 | Bed sheets |
| 4 | Dec 8, 2014 08:08 | Dec 8, 2014 10:17 | Mix program |
| 5 | Dec 9, 2014 07:36 | Dec 9, 2014 09:35 | Mix program |
| 6 | Dec 11, 2014 08:40 | Dec 11, 2014 10:47 | Mix program |
| 7 | Dec 15, 2014 17:02 | Dec 15, 2014 19:06 | Mix program |
| 8 | Dec 16, 2014 09:41 | Dec 16, 2014 11:41 | Sport cloths |
| 9 | Dec 16, 2014 13:00 | Dec 16, 2014 18:14 | Jeans |
| 10 | Dec 18, 2014 14:50 | Dec 18, 2014 18:49 | Bed sheets |

Source: Own illustration

Table 5: Intervals and magnitudes of characteristic drops of dryer

| Program | Repetition pattern | Drop magnitudes | End slot |
|---|---|---|---|
| Bed sheets | 31 s \| 61 s | 80 to 180 W | 4.5 min |
| Mix program | 62 s \| 1197 s | 80 to 180 W | 4.5 min |
| Sport cloths | 61 s \| 600 s | 80 to 180 W | 4.5 min |
| Jeans | 30 s \| 248 s | 110 to 250 W | 12 min |

Source: Own illustration

The reference data for the dryer was measured by the Volcraft Energy Logger 4000 with a one minute interval. While generating the reference data, the Volcraft created data gaps for no apparent reason. Fortunately, none of these gaps corresponded to times when the dryer was active. For completeness purposes, Table 6 shows the data gaps.

*Table 6: Data gaps of dryer reference data, generated by Volcraft logger*

| Start gap | End gap |
|---|---|
| Nov 27, 2014 00:00 | Nov 30, 2014 21:27 |
| Dec 6, 2014 21:15 | Dec 6, 2014 21:57 |
| Dec 12, 2014 17:35 | Dec 14, 2014 04:39 |

Source: Own illustration

## 4.1.2 Freezer (Phase 1)

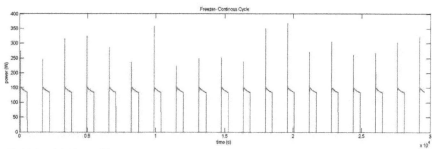

*Fig. 11: Sample load curve of freezer*

Source: Own illustration

Fig. 11 shows a sample of around 8 hours of the freezer in the test household. The appliance was produced by the firm Bauknecht as the model GT 2104 and it was connected to phase 1 of the household current. It is clearly visible that the freezer shows the characteristic continuous cycle of cooling appliances. Besides the high starting current and the slight power ramp-down, the appliance can be described as a two-state device, having an on-time and an off-time.

Usually the freezer cools for 8 to 9 minutes and consequently stays switched off for 16 to 18 minutes. If extensive cooling is needed, the cooling phase takes over some time of the off period. Thereby, the switch-on process happens relatively regularly every 25 minutes. The overshooting that happens when a cooling cycle starts varies greatly (among other things) due to the 1 second quantization. The peak value can be as little as 50W or as much as 350W above the stabilized starting value of 140W. After a small increase to 150W, a continuous decline to 130W starts before the on-cycle terminates.

The periodicity and the clear steps are the most striking characteristic of this device and thereby most promising for the single device recognition. The combination of step detection and estimating the area of a switch-on or switch-off event is promising.

*Table 7: Parameters of freezer cycle*

| | Overshooting | Initial Value | Peak Value | End Value | Off-cycle |
|---|---|---|---|---|---|
| **Watts** | 180 - 370 W | 140 W | 150 W | 130 W | 0 W |
| | 162 - 310 var | 162 var | 165 var | 162 var | 0 var |
| **Time** | after 1 - 3 s | after 2 - 4 s | after 45 s | after 8 to 9 min | Duration: 16 - 18 min |

**On-cycle**

Source: Own illustration

For the freezer, there was no reference data generated due to a lack of devices. However, since the freezer shows the cyclic nature in its power consumption, the location of the on and off switching events is pretty clear and can be proven manually.

### 4.1.3 Dishwasher (Phase 1)

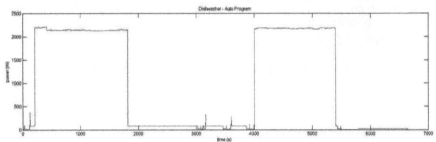

*Fig. 12: Sample load curve of dishwasher*
Source: Own illustration

Fig. 12 shows a sample washing cycle of a dishwasher. The appliance was produced by the firm Miele as the model Edition 111 W 5873 and it was connected to phase 1 of the household current. It is visible that the dishwasher is primarily a three-state device which is either switched off at zero watts, the initial or intermediate mode at 80W, or working at full power at 2100W. The graphic shows the automatic program (AP), which adapts to the amount of dishes inside. Although the time intervals changed within the AP and other settings like the energy efficiency program (EEP), the basic pattern of two full power and an intermediate slot are always valid. In some rare cases, the power drops to the 80W for half a minute before continuing at full power after the first minute of the second on-cycle.

The on-cycles of the dishwasher can last between 12 to 20 minutes for the EEP and 18 to 32 minutes for the AP. The intermediate slot is 60 to 66 minutes for the EEP and 12 to 38 minutes for the AP. The runtime before and after the first and last on- and off-cycle is constant, which helps to extrapolate the start and end time from the state transition from low to full power. The low power state before the first on-cycle lasts 95s for the AP and 555s for the EEP. The proceeding runtime is 30s for the AP and 300s for the EEP.

These patterns can be used to detect the appliance in the household. Even if similar jumps in power can be produced by different appliances, iterating through the criteria makes a false detection basically impossible. A jump in power always has to be followed by a suiting drop to form a pair, and two consecutive pairs are only allowed to be separated by a certain period of intermediate time to mark an event.

*Table 8: Parameters of dishwasher event*

|  | Start slot | First cycle | Intermediate | Second cycle | End slot |
|---|---|---|---|---|---|
| **Watts** | 80 W | 2100 W | 80 W | 2100 W | 80 W |
|  | 8 var | 0 var | 10 var | 0 var | 10 var |
| **Time** | AP: 95 s | AP: 12 – 20 min | AP: 12 – 38 min | AP: 12 – 20 min | AP: 30 s |
|  | EEP: 555 s | EEP: 18 – 38 min | EEP: 60 – 66 min | EEP: 18 – 38 min | EEP: 300 s |

Source: Own illustration

For the test period, the following events were detected:

Table 9: Dishwasher events during test period

| # | Start | End | Program |
|---|-------|-----|---------|
| 1 | Nov 28, 2014 08:22 | Nov 28, 2014 10:12 | Energy efficiency program |
| 2 | Nov 30, 2014 21:46 | Nov 30, 2014 22:55 | Automatic program |
| 3 | Dec 4, 2014 23:11 | Dec 5, 2014 00:43 | Automatic program |
| 4 | Dec 8, 2014 00:34 | Dec 8, 2014 01:31 | Automatic program |
| 5 | Dec 11, 2014 07:03 | Dec 11, 2014 08:19 | Automatic program |
| 6 | Dec 14, 2014 16:43 | Dec 14 2014 17:51 | Automatic program |
| 7 | Dec 17, 2014 08:12 | Dec 17, 2014 09:11 | Automatic program |

Source: Own illustration

The reference data for the dryer was measured by the CLM1000 presented in Chapter 3. For this purpose, only one minute intervals were used. The data could be generated without data gaps.

## 4.2    Analysis of Overall Load Data

This paragraph provides an example of the data, which was generated over the interface of the Berg meter, described in Chapter 3.

The figures are plotted from the real power values of the test data to act as an example. The week from Monday December 1, until Sunday, December 7, 2014 was selected and important events were marked. The red boxes contain events from the dryer, the green box the ones of the dishwasher. Having the prior information about the load curve of the different appliances presented in the former section, one is still able to recognize the phases the appliances are connected to and their cycles. Comparing the single phases to the aggregated total power, this already becomes a lot harder. The purple boxes illustrate two samples of phase 3, where there is almost no other device active than the continuous running freezer. Taking a closer look, the pattern can be seen throughout the whole sample of a week.

The data was measured from November 27, 2014 00:00:00 until December 18, 2014 23:59:59, which corresponds to 22 days. Since the produced raw data was relatively big in size, the data generation was interrupted a few times to save the data block and start a new measurement one minute later. In addition to this planned data gaps, there was one issue with the logging laptop, which lead to a gap of a few hours. Fortunately, no events of the dishwasher and dryer occurred during that time. In addition, there was no state change for the freezer in the one minute gaps and only full cycles were hidden by the gap of 9 hours.

The produced data gaps and the states of the AOIs are marked in the following table:

Table 10: Data gaps and states of AOIs

| Start gap | End gap | State dishwasher | State freezer | State dryer |
|-----------|---------|------------------|---------------|-------------|
| Nov 30, 2014 19:03:00 | Nov 30, 2014 19:03:59 | Off \| Off | Off \| Off | Off \| Off |
| Dec 6, 2014 12:23:00 | Dec 6, 2014 12:23:59 | Off \| Off | Off \| Off | Off \| Off |
| Dec 9, 2014 23:45:00 | Dec 10, 2014 08:37:59 | Off \| Off | Off \| Off | Off \| Off |
| Dec 14, 2014 10:48:00 | Dec 14, 2014 10:48:59 | Off \| Off | On \| On | Off \| Off |

Source: Own illustration

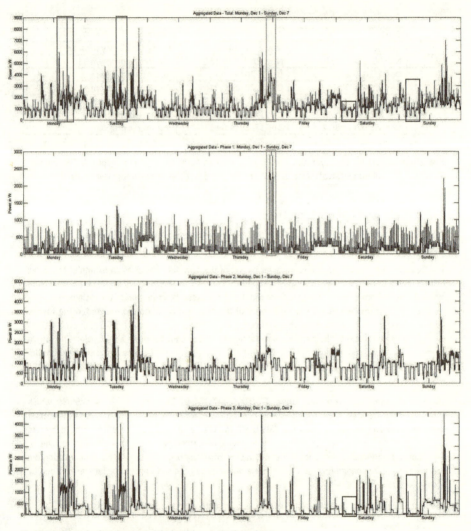

*Fig. 13: Week sample of total power and the breakdown in the three phases*

Source: Own illustration

# 5.   Detection Algorithm

The previous chapter analyzed the overall load data and the signatures of individual appliances. Some of the characteristics of the single devices were visible in the aggregated data, which motivated an approach of post-processing disaggregation. This would lead to significant simplification in comparison to measuring every single appliance with a meter right at the power outlet. Therefore, computational algorithms to perform energy disaggregation or NALM have attracted research for some years, as already shown in the Chapters 1 and 2. An important criterion for the development of an algorithm is the dataset available to it. On the one hand, having current, voltage, and reactive power in addition to the real power can make a difference. On the other hand, the granularity of the data is a critical issue. A publication of Armel et al. shows the need of higher frequency sampling to enable a fully disaggregated energy consumption [6].

As already stated, this thesis will focus on data available over smart meters, since this approach sensibly leverages a hardware infrastructure which will be available in the future in basically every household. Chapter 2 described the general concept of a smart meter and the structure which will be used in Germany within the "Messsysteme 2020" project. The used meter of the firm Berg GmbH and its characteristics, as well as the whole measurement and logging setup, were described in Chapter 3. The test data was generated with this hardware and its characteristics were analyzed in the previous Chapter 4. Due to the characteristics of the different appliances, different algorithm approaches evolve.

## 5.1   Assessment Criteria for Algorithms

Before explaining the developed algorithm approaches, the assessment criteria will be fixed. To clarify the notification used, the variables are explained in the following table:

Table 11: Description of used notation

| Variable | Meaning | Example |
|---|---|---|
| $C_1$ | Criterion 1 | $N = 2, N_{NALM,C_2=0} = 1, \rightarrow C_1 = 50$ |
| $C_2$ | Criterion 2 | $N = 2, N_{NALM,C_1=0} = 3, \rightarrow C_2 = 50$ |
| $C_3$ | Criterion 3 | $\vec{X} = \begin{pmatrix} 120 \\ 1267 \end{pmatrix}, \vec{Y} = \begin{pmatrix} 272 \\ 1437 \end{pmatrix}, \vec{X}_{NALM,C_1=0,C_2=0} = \begin{pmatrix} 120 \\ 1265 \end{pmatrix}, \vec{Y}_{NALM,C_1=0,C_2=0} = \begin{pmatrix} 272 \\ 1437 \end{pmatrix}, \rightarrow C_3 = \frac{2}{2} = 1$ |
| $C_4$ | Criterion 4 | $\vec{T} = \begin{pmatrix} 152 \\ 170 \end{pmatrix}, \vec{T}_{NALM,C_1=0,C_2=0} = \begin{pmatrix} 152 \\ 172 \end{pmatrix}, \rightarrow C_4 = \frac{0+\frac{2}{170}}{2} = 0{,}006$ |
| $N$ | Number (No.) of events | $N = 2$ |
| $N_{NALM}$ | No. of events detected (det.) by algorithm (algo.) | $N_{NALM} = 2$ |
| $N_{NALM,C_1=0}$ | No. of events det. by algo., fulfilling $C_1$ | $N_{NALM,C_1=0} = 3$ |
| $N_{NALM,C_2=0}$ | No. of events det. by algo., fulfilling $C_2$ | $N_{NALM,C_2=0} = 1$ |
| $\vec{T}$ | Durations of events (all in min.) | $\vec{T} = \vec{Y} - \vec{X} = \begin{pmatrix} 152 \\ 170 \end{pmatrix}$ |
| $\vec{T}_{NALM,C_1=0,C_2=0}$ | Durations of det. events, fulfilling $C_1$ and $C_2$ | $\vec{T}_{NALM,C_1=0,C_2=0} = \vec{Y}_{NALM,C_1=0,C_2=0} - \vec{X}_{NALM,C_1=0,C_2=0} = \begin{pmatrix} 152 \\ 172 \end{pmatrix}$ |

| $\vec{X}$ | Start times of events (all in min., starting from base time) | $\vec{X} = \begin{pmatrix} 120 \\ 1267 \end{pmatrix}$ |
|---|---|---|
| $\vec{X}_{NALM}$ | Start times of det. Events | $\vec{X}_{NALM} = \begin{pmatrix} 613 \\ 1265 \end{pmatrix}$ |
| $\vec{X}_{NALM,C_1=0,C_2=0}$ | Start times of det. events, fulfilling $C_1$ and $C_2$ | $\vec{X}_{NALM,C_1=0} = \begin{pmatrix} 120 \\ 613 \\ 1265 \end{pmatrix}, \vec{X}_{NALM,C_2=0} = (1265),$ $\vec{X}_{NALM,C_1=0,C_2=0} = \begin{pmatrix} 120 \\ 1265 \end{pmatrix}$ |
| $\vec{Y}$ | Stop times of events | $\vec{Y} = \begin{pmatrix} 272 \\ 1437 \end{pmatrix}$ |
| $\vec{Y}_{NALM}$ | Stop times of det. events | $\vec{Y}_{NALM} = \begin{pmatrix} 762 \\ 1437 \end{pmatrix}$ |
| $\vec{Y}_{NALM,C_1=0,C_2=0}$ | Stop times of det. events, fulfilling $C_1$ and $C_2$ | $\vec{X}_{NALM,C_1=0} = \begin{pmatrix} 272 \\ 762 \\ 1437 \end{pmatrix}, \vec{X}_{NALM,C_2=0} = (1437),$ $\vec{X}_{NALM,C_1=0,C_2=0} = \begin{pmatrix} 272 \\ 1437 \end{pmatrix}$ |

Source: Own illustration

The following four criteria serve as a basic evaluation point to rate the performance of the algorithms.

The first criterion displays, how many of the complete events or on-cycles could not be successfully detected.

**Definition criterion 1:** *The first criterion describes the percentage value of how many of the complete events or cycles N could not be successfully detected. The value $N_{NALM,C_2=0}$ is the already corrected version of $N_{NALM}$ in the sense that the potential false detections are already eliminated ($C_2 = 0$).*

**Formula criterion 1:**

$$C_1 = \frac{N - N_{NALM,C_2=0}}{N} * 100$$

The second criterion consequently indicates, how many of the complete events or on-cycles were detected by mistake.

**Definition criterion 2:** *The second criterion describes the percentage value of how many of the detected complete events or cycles $N_{NALM,C_1=0}$ were detected by mistake. The value $N_{NALM,C_1=0}$ is the already corrected version of $N_{NALM}$ in the sense that potential missing events were already added according to N ($C_1 = 0$).*

**Formula criterion 2:**

$$C_2 = \frac{N_{NALM,C_1=0} - N}{N} * 100$$

The third criterion marks how accurately the algorithm is working. The difference in minutes of the start event and the stop event are added to gain the total delta. Furthermore, the average is taken.

**Definition criterion 3:** *The third criterion describes the average deviation of the postulated start value vector $\vec{X}_{NALM,C_1=0,C_2=0}$ and the stop value vector $\vec{Y}_{NALM,C_1=0,C_2=0}$ from the true values aggregated in $\vec{X}$ and $\vec{Y}$. The values $\vec{X}_{NALM,C_1=0,C_2=0}$ and $\vec{Y}_{NALM,C_1=0,C_2=0}$ are already corrected according to the criteria $C_1$ and $C_2$. $C_3$ is calculated by building the average of the N total deviations. The total deviation is created by adding the difference in the start and stop time.*

**Formula criterion 3:**

$$C_3 = \frac{\sum_{i=1}^{N} \left| X_{NALM,C_1=0,C_2=0,i} - X_i \right| + \left| Y_{NALM,C_1=0,C_2=0,i} - Y_i \right|}{N}$$

The fourth criterion evaluates, whether the runtime of the event or cycle of an appliance is detected correctly.

**Definition criterion 4:** *The fourth criterion compares the calculated runtimes from the algorithm output, aggregated in the vector $\vec{T}_{NALM,C_1=0,C_2=0}$, with the reference data runtimes vector $\vec{T}$. The average percentage of the relative errors of the N events is used to create $C_4$.*

**Formula criterion 4:**

$$C_4 = \frac{\sum_{i=1}^{N} \frac{T_{NALM,C_1=0,C_2=0,i} - T_i}{T_i} * 100}{N}$$

## 5.2 Algorithm Design

Generally, NALM approaches can be divided into two kinds of methods according to their data granularity [24]. High-frequency data sampling of kHz motivates an analysis of the waveform or higher harmonics using a transformation in the frequency domain (e.g. Froehlich et al. [7]). In contrast, low-frequency methods take the load profiles into account [24]. Since the used setup belongs to the latter group, the three algorithm designs are relying on the generated data without any further frequency transformation. The basic idea of using steps in the real power P and the reactive power Q was already used by Hart as shown in Chapter 2. However, the three algorithm designs introduce new features, which work successfully in detecting the AOIs. The following paragraphs will introduce the designs of the three different approaches.

### 5.2.1 Algorithm Design 1: PQ Steps with Cycle Length Detection

The first algorithm approach was implemented to detect the on-cycles of the freezer. Generally, every cooling device follows the similar pattern of a cyclic two-state device. It switches on at a certain point of time and stays on until the reference temperature is reached. The variation of the on-cycle mostly depends on the groceries in the freezer, changes in the surrounding environment, and the frequency of usage.

Since the content of the freezer is not changed too often, it is based in the cellar of the house, and it is not frequently used, the cycles of the device are relatively constant. This is really valuable for the implementation of the algorithm. As already shown in Table 7, the freezer switches on with a step of 140 W and 162 var and switches off with 130 W and 162 var. These input parameters along with an initial tolerance of 10 % around these values are used for the algorithm. The necessary cycle length is detected during runtime and the program allows a 20 % tolerance around it. In the following, the pseudo code of the script will be provided.

Pseudo code of algorithm 1: PQ Steps with cycle length detection

1. Find all on- and off-steps within the initial tolerance
2. Detect standard cycle length by iteration and elimination of outliers
3. Check if device is already switched on at beginning or is still running at the end
4. Pair on- and off-steps and find areas of missing entries
5. Postulate location of missing entries with cycle length and increase the tolerance locally
6. Choose candidate with best likelihood approach
7. Set postulated value if step was hidden by parallel transition of devices (error!)
8. Return on- and off-cycles

## 5.2.2 Algorithm Design 2: P Steps with Event Duration Consideration

The second algorithm approach was implemented to detect the events of the dishwasher. Since the full power phase of the dishwasher does not include reactive power and also the other phases show only a little amount of that quantity, the former step detection in the P and Q domain does not make sense. While the discrete steps in the real power are already a good indicator, another feature is necessary to avoid false detections of any similar steps in real power.

The dishwasher is basically a three-state device with a significant step in real power of around 2020 W from low power (80 W) to full power (2100 W) mode. In addition, the different washing programs all follow a similar behavior as outlined in Chapter 4. The appearance of two similar on-cycles, separated by an interval of a certain range is sufficient to detect the appliance. The program uses the outlined 2020 W as the rise and fall step as well as a 10 % initial tolerance as input parameters. Furthermore, the information about the event duration is hard coded. In the following, the pseudo code of the script will be provided.

Pseudo code of algorithm 2: P Steps with event duration consideration

1. Find all on- and off-steps within certain tolerance
2. Pair on- and off-steps, if they happened within a certain interval
3. Pair on-cycles if they happened separated by a certain intermediate interval
4. Detect the mode (AP or EEP) and take the corresponding start and end slot into account
5. Return start and end of event

## 5.2.3 Algorithm Design 3: PQ Steps with Runtime Pattern Analysis

The third algorithm approach was implemented to detect the events of the dryer. As shown in Chapter 4, all of the drying programs show characteristic drops in power, which happen in discrete intervals. Detecting these intervals helps to exactly determine which program is used and indicate the rough time when the dryer is turned on and off. Using the larger PQ steps with some additional parameters as shown in the previous section helps to exactly determine the start and end time.

The algorithm relies on the data shown in Table 5. An average switch-on step of 440 W and 220 var, as well as a switch-off step of 980 W and 330 var serve as input parameters. To cover all the different drying programs, a tolerance of 40 % was allowed. This was not a major problem, since the estimated event region could already be narrowed down significantly, leaving little probability of false detections. For the detection of the drops, a wide cluster of 160 W (respectively 210 W for the jeans program) with

50% tolerance was used. However, due to the necessity of a direct recess after an initial drop, not many false detections occur.

In the following, the pseudo code of the script will be provided.

Pseudo code of algorithm 3: PQ Steps with runtime pattern analysis

1. Find all drops with consecutive positive steps in given cluster
2. Measure intervals between events
3. Eliminate obvious redundant events during estimated runtime of appliance
4. Test intervals vector against characteristic parameters
5. Detect program used and define possible start and stop event interval
6. Detect PQ steps and take the corresponding start and end slot into account
7. Return start and end of events

## 5.3 Result of Algorithms on Test Data

The following section describes the results of the algorithms presented in the section above while applied on the generated test data. In addition to providing the output of the script, the defined assessment criteria are used to rate the performance.

### 5.3.1 Results of Algorithm Design 1

The first algorithm approach was intended to detect the events of the freezer in the test household.

The whole output data is provided in the appendix. It was able to register every single one of the 1112 full cycles and detect the switch-off event of the already running freezer in the beginning of the test time. The cycle length auto detection generated 1680 s or 28 min as the average interval. In only one case there was the actual need to follow step 7 of the provided pseudo code and postulate an event. This was the case for a switch-off event at 1,070,796 (2014-12-9 9:26:35) which was set to 1,070,806 (2014-12-9 9:26:45). The reason why the event could not be detected is that it was hidden by an unlikely simultaneous switch-off of another device with higher power. In addition to performing a sanity analysis on the data, the whole data set was plotted with the applied algorithm and checked manually for other missing entries.

Since there were no other errors found manually either way, it can be assumed that every other cycle was successfully detected. In addition, since the cluster expansion was only done locally, it is very unlikely that a correct step was hidden and an incorrect one was randomly present within this short time frame. As seen in the error case mentioned above, returning an error instead of a false entry is more common. Therefore, it is valid to assume that the steps were measured perfectly aligned and therefore definitely refer to the right minute. Even in the case of the error, the 10 seconds offset was within the granularity used for this analysis. As not a whole cycle had to be postulated but just a single event, the algorithm still reaches a perfect score within the assessment criteria.

Table 12: Expected results of algorithm 1: detection of freezer

| Criterion | Result |
|---|---|
| $C_1$ | 0 |
| $C_2$ | 0 |
| $C_3$ | 0 |
| $C_4$ | 0 |

Source: Own illustration

## 5.3.2   Results of Algorithm Design 2

The second algorithm approach was intended to detect the events of the dishwasher in the test household.

In the following, the output of the Matlab test script of algorithm 2 is provided in a slightly formatted version.

```
Dishwasher On/Off Events
        On          |          Off
2014-11-28, 08:22   |   2014-11-28, 10:12
2014-11-30, 21:46   |   2014-11-30, 22:53
2014-12-04, 23:11   |   2014-12-05, 00:43
2014-12-08, 00:34   |   2014-12-08, 01:31
2014-12-11, 07:03   |   2014-12-11, 08:20
2014-12-14, 16:44   |   2014-12-14, 17:52
2014-12-17, 08:13   |   2014-12-17, 09:12
```

Table 13 shows a comparison of the output of the algorithm and the reference values. The last column provides the variation of the detected event times in minutes, aggregated from the start and end difference. This deviation is used for the assessment criterion 3.

Table 13: Comparison of algorithm 2 output to reference

| # | Start reference | Algorithm | End reference | Algorithm | Total delta |
|---|---|---|---|---|---|
| 1 | 2014-11-28, 08:22 | 2014-11-28, 08:22 | 2014-11-28, 10:12 | 2014-11-28, 10:12 | 0 |
| 2 | 2014-11-30, 21:46 | 2014-11-30, 21:46 | 2014-11-30, 22:55 | 2014-11-30, 22:53 | 2 |
| 3 | 2014-12-04, 23:11 | 2014-12-04, 23:11 | 2014-12-05, 00:43 | 2014-12-05, 00:43 | 0 |
| 4 | 2014-12-08, 00:34 | 2014-12-08, 00:34 | 2014-12-08, 01:31 | 2014-12-08, 01:31 | 0 |
| 5 | 2014-12-11, 07:03 | 2014-12-11, 07:03 | 2014-12-11, 08:19 | 2014-12-11, 08:20 | 1 |
| 6 | 2014-12-14, 16:43 | 2014-12-14, 16:44 | 2014-12-14, 17:51 | 2014-12-14, 17:52 | 2 |
| 7 | 2014-12-17, 08:12 | 2014-12-17, 08:13 | 2014-12-17, 09:11 | 2014-12-17, 09:12 | 2 |

Source: Own illustration

Table 14 shows the results of applying the assessment criteria to the output of algorithm 2. The algorithm detects every event very precisely. The estimated time of start and end events matches in 57 % of the cases and there is never more than a 2 minutes total delta in all the 7 events.

Table 14: Results of algorithm 2: detection of dishwasher

| Criteria | Results |
|---|---|
| $C_1$ | 0 |
| $C_2$ | 0 |
| $C_3$ | 1 |
| $C_4$ | 0.60 |

Source: Own illustration

## 5.3.3   Results of Algorithm Design 3

The third algorithm approach was intended to detect the events of the dryer in the test household.

In the following, the output of the Matlab test script of algorithm 3 is provided in a slightly formatted version.

Dryer On/Off Events

| On | | Off |
|---|---|---|
| Bed sheets program: | | |
| 2014-12-01, 14:02 | | 2014-12-01, 16:50 |
| 2014-12-02, 12:53 | | 2014-12-02, 15:44 |
| 2014-12-18, 14:50 | | 2014-12-18, 18:50 |
| Mix program: | | |
| 2014-12-01, 17:39 | | 2014-12-01, 19:08 |
| 2014-12-08, 08:06 | | 2014-12-08, 10:17 |
| 2014-12-09, 07:36 | | 2014-12-09, 09:36 |
| 2014-12-11, 08:40 | | 2014-12-11, 10:47 |
| 2014-12-15, 17:02 | | 2014-12-15, 19:06 |
| Jeans program: | | |
| 2014-12-16, 13:01 | | 2014-12-16, 18:15 |
| Sport program: | | |
| 2014-12-16, 09:41 | | 2014-12-16, 11:42 |

Table 15 shows a comparison of the output of the algorithm and the reference values, as already shown in the previous section. Again, the last column provides the variation of the detected event times in minutes, aggregated from the start and end difference. This deviation is used for the assessment criterion 3.

Table 15: Comparison of algorithm 3 output to reference

| # | Start reference | Algorithm | End reference | Algorithm | Total delta |
|---|---|---|---|---|---|
| 1 | 2014-12-01, 14:02 | 2014-12-01, 14:02 | 2014-12-01, 16:50 | 2014-12-01, 16:50 | 0 |
| 2 | 2014-12-01, 17:40 | 2014-12-01, 17:39 | 2014-12-01, 19:07 | 2014-12-01, 19:08 | 2 |
| 3 | 2014-12-02, 12:54 | 2014-12-02, 12:53 | 2014-12-02, 15:44 | 2014-12-02, 15:44 | 1 |
| 4 | 2014-12-08, 08:08 | 2014-12-08, 08:06 | 2014-12-08, 10:17 | 2014-12-08, 10:17 | 2 |
| 5 | 2014-12-09, 07:36 | 2014-12-09, 07:36 | 2014-12-09, 09:35 | 2014-12-09, 09:36 | 1 |
| 6 | 2014-12-11, 08:40 | 2014-12-11, 08:40 | 2014-12-11, 10:47 | 2014-12-11, 10:47 | 0 |
| 7 | 2014-12-15, 17:02 | 2014-12-15, 17:02 | 2014-12-15, 19:06 | 2014-12-15, 19:06 | 0 |
| 8 | 2014-12-15, 09:41 | 2014-12-15, 09:41 | 2014-12-15, 11:41 | 2014-12-15, 11:42 | 1 |
| 9 | 2014-12-16, 13:00 | 2014-12-16, 13:01 | 2014-12-16, 18:14 | 2014-12-16, 18:15 | 2 |
| 10 | 2014-12-18, 14:50 | 2014-12-18, 14:50 | 2014-12-18, 18:49 | 2014-12-18, 18:50 | 1 |

Source: Own illustration

Table 16 shows the results of applying the assessment criteria to the output of algorithm 3. The algorithm detects every event very precisely. The estimated time matches in 55 % of the cases and there is never more than a 2 minutes total delta in all the 10 events. In this case, algorithm 3 shows a better performance according to the fourth criterion than algorithm 2. In addition, the prediction of the drying program used in the different cases worked with a 100 % certainty.

Table 16: Results of algorithm 3: detection of dryer

| Criteria | Results |
|---|---|
| $C_1$ | 0 |
| $C_2$ | 0 |
| $C_3$ | 1 |
| $C_4$ | 0.52 |

Source: Own illustration

# 6. Enhancement Options of the Program

## 6.1 Response to the Research Question

This Bachelor thesis dealt with the research question of how reliable home appliances can be detected from data generated from smart meters and which methods are the most promising ones. The data generation was successfully implemented, leveraging the RS-485 interface of the smart meter and communicating over the Modbus RTU protocol. A script was created to process the data and deliver a suiting format. Meanwhile, algorithms were developed and trained by the parameters extracted from the individual load curves of the appliances. Promising approaches were the detection of steps in the real and reactive power in combination with three different characteristics: the duration of certain events, the cyclic nature of an appliance, and the analysis of a runtime pattern. This enables the detection of more complex devices (e.g. the dryer) with more than two states. Other transformations of pattern recognition in the frequency domain were not used due to the low-frequency sampling of 1 Hz in the test setting.

The three algorithms performed very well for their appliance group. Every event of the three AOIs could successfully be detected and the time deviation on a minute scale was negligible. Although the programs were trained on the characteristics of the specific appliances in the test environment, the parameters could be easily adapted to different devices. Therefore, the approaches seem to be very promising to be applicable in a variety of locations and use cases.

## 6.2 Improvement Possibilities

Since the focus was on the development of an algorithm, the implemented function is not perfectly user friendly. Integrating the algorithms into a program with a graphical user interface, which enables the creation of plots, visualization of the runtime of an AOI, and other functions, would deliver a valuable product. In addition, instead of using three different scripts with the algorithms, a logic could be implemented, where the program decides, which approach is best suited for the occasion. Generally, the program could be extended to new classes of appliances to cover most of the energy consumption in a household. By generating one single appliance load curve, the necessary parameters could automatically be extracted from the data. One should only be obligated to provide the raw data from the single appliance and the smart meter, while the program aggregates all the necessary data automatically. An example algorithm could follow these steps: First, identify the largest steps in power from the single appliance load curve. Second, check if the events occurred within a feasible time. Third, use found parameters to perform the detection process on the overall data.

Driving the scenario to the optimum, one could imagine the AS-NALM Hart already referred to in his early work [4]. A plug-and-play solution without the necessity of training the algorithm with single appliance data could be the ultimate break-through in the case of user friendliness. This would require the program to experience a learning phase, where it aggregates data, identifies pattern, proves the assumption, and iterates. The easiest device group would be the cooling appliances due to their cyclic pattern. In the algorithm presented in this thesis, the cycle length was already learned. By repeating the process with different real and reactive power clusters, striking correlations could be detected.

There are already start-ups, which claim to have a hardware and software combination that is able to disaggregate the overall data in a household. Verdigris is using higher harmonics with up to 15 kHz, measured by their customized hardware [25]. However, they rely on an immense database, where reference appliances are listed. Thereby, the system is only learns a few things while operating, which makes it more MS-NALM than AS-NALM. What Verdigris already does and what would be really valuable for a potential end consumer is the extrapolation of the energy consumption instead of providing only the switch-on and switch-off events of an appliance. Thereby, the user would know, how much every device in the household approximately consumes and which appliance is worth replacing by a new version. This ultimately leads to more awareness and reduced energy consumption, which was a major motivation of this thesis in the first place.

# Acknowledgements

I want to thank everybody, who supported me during the work on this thesis.

First of all I want to thank Prof. Dr.-Ing. Diepold as the professor in charge of supporting this particular research at his Chair of Data Processing of the Technische Universität München.

Second, I want to thank my two advisors Julian Habigt of the Technische Universität München and Max Engelken of the Center of Digital Technology and Management for their support, professional input, and valuable meetings. The technical discussions and instructions on professional work contributed significantly to the success of the thesis.

Last but not least, I want to thank my parents for their unconditional support. Their house served as the test household and was thereby changed into a test environment. I want to especially thank my mother for supporting me with the generation of the test data.

# References

[1]     *B23/B24 Benutzerhandbuch*, 1st ed., Berg GmbH,: Martinsried, DEU, 2013, pp. 1-166.
[2]     *Digitus USB to serial RS485 converter.* , ASSMANN Electron. GmbH,: Luedenscheid, DEU, 2014, pp. 1-16.
[3]     *Fieldtalk modpoll*, 3.4 ed., ProconX Pty Ltd.,: Sumner, AUS, 2013, pp. 1-3.
[4]     G. W. Hart, "Nonintrusive appliance load monitoring," *Proc. IEEE,* vol. 80, no. 12, pp. 1870-1891, Dec. 1992.
[5]     S. Darby, "The effectiveness of feedback on energy consumption," Environmental Change Inst., Oxford, GBR, Review Apr. 2006.
[6]     C. K. Armel et al., "Disaggregation: the holy grail of energy efficiency," Precourt Energy Efficiency Center, Stanford, CA, Rep. May 2012.
[7]     J. Froehlich et al., "Disaggregated end-use energy sensing for the smart grid," IEEE Comput. Soc., Washington D.C., USA, Article Mar. 2011.
[8]     Deutsche Energie-Agentur GmbH, "Einführung von Smart Meter in Deutschland," dena, Berlin, DEU, Study Jul. 2014.
[9]     The Climate Group, "Smart 2020: Enabling the low carbon economy in the information age," Global eSustainability Init., London, GBR, Rep. 2008.
[10]    Bundesamt für Sicherheit in der Informationstechnik, "Das Smart Meter Gateway," BSI, Bonn, DEU, Brochure BSI-Bro14/332, Feb. 2014.
[11]    *Energiewirtschaftsgesetz § 21c - Einbau von Messsystemen,* Federal Government of Germany, 2010.
[12]    Forum Netztechnik/Netzbetrieb im VDE, "Projekt „MessSystem 2020" - Eckpunkte," FNN, Berlin, DEU, Brochure Jul. 2012.
[13]    G. W. Hart, "Prototype nonintrusive appliance monitor," MIT Energy Laboratory, Concord, MA, Progress Rep. Sep. 1985.
[14]    G. W. Hart, "Residential energy monitoring and computerized surveillance via utility power," *IEEE Technol. Soc. Mag.,* vol. 8, no. 2, pp. 12-16, Jun. 1989.
[15]    S. Drenker and A. Kader, "Nonintrusive monitoring of electric loads," *IEEE Computer Applicat. Power,* vol. 12, no. 4, pp. 47-51, Oct. 1999.
[16]    C. Laughman et al., "Power signature analysis," *IEEE Power Energy Mag.,* vol. 1, no. 2, pp. 56-63, Apr. 2003.
[17]    F. Sultanem, "Using appliance signatures for monitoring residential loads at meter panal level," *IEEE Trans. Power Del.,* vol. 6, no. 4, pp. 1380-1385, Oct. 1991.
[18]    J. G. Roos et al., "Using neural networks for non-intrusive monitoring of industrial electrical loads," in *Proc. IEEE Instrumentation and Measurement Technology Conf.,* Hamamatsu, JPN, 1994, pp. 1115-1118.
[19]    J. Z. Kolter and M. J. Johnsin, "REDD - a public data set for energy disaggregation research," in *Proc. SustKDD Workshop on Data Mining Applications in Sustainability,* San Diego, CA, 2011, pp. 1-6.
[20]    K. Anderson et al., "BLUED - a fully labeled public dataset for event-based non-intrusive load monitoring research," in *Proc. 2nd KDD Workshop on Data Mining Applications in Sustainability,* Beijing, CHN, 2012, pp. 2-16.
[21]    Modbus.org, "MODBUS over serial line," Specification, Dec. 2006.
[22]    B&B Electronics Manufacturing Company, "RS-485 connections FAQ," B&B Electron. Mfg. Co., Ottawa, IL, Tech. Article 2013.
[23]    *CLM1000 Professional Bedienungsanleitung*, 4th ed., Christ-Elektronik GmbH,: Memmingen, DEU, 2014.
[24]    G. Eibl and D. Engel, "Influence of data granularity on nonintrusive appliance load monitoring," in *Proc. 2nd ACM Workshop on Information Hiding and Multimedia Security,* Salzburg, AUT, 2014, pp. 147-151.

[25]    M. Chung, "Non-intrusive load monitoring," Verdigris Technol., Moffett Field, CA, Whitepaper Jan. 2014.

# Appendix

## List of Figures

## List of Tables

Details on CRC Generation [21]

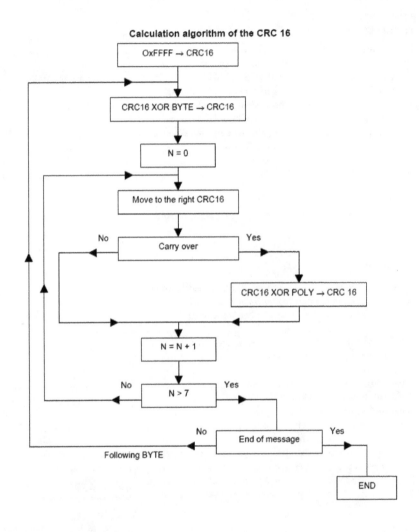

**Calculation algorithm of the CRC 16**

OxFFFF → CRC16

CRC16 XOR BYTE → CRC16

N = 0

Move to the right CRC16

Carry over

No                                    Yes

CRC16 XOR POLY → CRC 16

N = N + 1

No            N > 7            Yes

No        End of message        Yes

Following BYTE

END

# Output Algorithm Design 1

Freezer On/Off Events

| On | Off |
| --- | --- |
| 2014-11-27, 0: 0 | 2014-11-27, 0: 2 |
| 2014-11-27, 0:24 | 2014-11-27, 0:32 |
| 2014-11-27, 0:53 | 2014-11-27, 1: 1 |
| 2014-11-27, 1:22 | 2014-11-27, 1:30 |
| 2014-11-27, 1:52 | 2014-11-27, 2: 0 |
| 2014-11-27, 2:21 | 2014-11-27, 2:29 |
| 2014-11-27, 2:51 | 2014-11-27, 2:59 |
| 2014-11-27, 3:20 | 2014-11-27, 3:28 |
| 2014-11-27, 3:50 | 2014-11-27, 3:58 |
| 2014-11-27, 4:19 | 2014-11-27, 4:27 |
| 2014-11-27, 4:49 | 2014-11-27, 4:57 |
| 2014-11-27, 5:18 | 2014-11-27, 5:26 |
| 2014-11-27, 5:48 | 2014-11-27, 5:56 |
| 2014-11-27, 6:18 | 2014-11-27, 6:26 |
| 2014-11-27, 6:47 | 2014-11-27, 6:55 |
| 2014-11-27, 7:17 | 2014-11-27, 7:25 |
| 2014-11-27, 7:46 | 2014-11-27, 7:54 |
| 2014-11-27, 8:16 | 2014-11-27, 8:24 |
| 2014-11-27, 8:45 | 2014-11-27, 8:54 |
| 2014-11-27, 9:15 | 2014-11-27, 9:23 |
| 2014-11-27, 9:45 | 2014-11-27, 9:53 |
| 2014-11-27, 10:15 | 2014-11-27, 10:23 |
| 2014-11-27, 10:44 | 2014-11-27, 10:52 |
| 2014-11-27, 11:13 | 2014-11-27, 11:21 |
| 2014-11-27, 11:43 | 2014-11-27, 11:51 |
| 2014-11-27, 12:12 | 2014-11-27, 12:20 |
| 2014-11-27, 12:41 | 2014-11-27, 12:49 |
| 2014-11-27, 13:10 | 2014-11-27, 13:18 |
| 2014-11-27, 13:40 | 2014-11-27, 13:48 |
| 2014-11-27, 14: 9 | 2014-11-27, 14:17 |
| 2014-11-27, 14:39 | 2014-11-27, 14:47 |
| 2014-11-27, 15: 8 | 2014-11-27, 15:16 |
| 2014-11-27, 15:37 | 2014-11-27, 15:45 |
| 2014-11-27, 16: 6 | 2014-11-27, 16:14 |
| 2014-11-27, 16:36 | 2014-11-27, 16:44 |
| 2014-11-27, 17: 6 | 2014-11-27, 17:13 |
| 2014-11-27, 17:35 | 2014-11-27, 17:43 |
| 2014-11-27, 18: 4 | 2014-11-27, 18:12 |
| 2014-11-27, 18:34 | 2014-11-27, 18:42 |
| 2014-11-27, 19: 3 | 2014-11-27, 19:11 |
| 2014-11-27, 19:32 | 2014-11-27, 19:40 |
| 2014-11-27, 20: 1 | 2014-11-27, 20: 9 |
| 2014-11-27, 20:29 | 2014-11-27, 20:37 |
| 2014-11-27, 20:58 | 2014-11-27, 21: 6 |
| 2014-11-27, 21:27 | 2014-11-27, 21:35 |
| 2014-11-27, 21:57 | 2014-11-27, 22: 5 |
| 2014-11-27, 22:27 | 2014-11-27, 22:35 |
| 2014-11-27, 22:56 | 2014-11-27, 23: 5 |
| 2014-11-27, 23:26 | 2014-11-27, 23:33 |
| 2014-11-27, 23:55 | 2014-11-28, 0: 3 |
| 2014-11-28, 0:24 | 2014-11-28, 0:32 |
| 2014-11-28, 0:53 | 2014-11-28, 1: 1 |
| 2014-11-28, 1:22 | 2014-11-28, 1:30 |
| 2014-11-28, 1:52 | 2014-11-28, 2: 0 |
| 2014-11-28, 2:21 | 2014-11-28, 2:29 |
| 2014-11-28, 2:50 | 2014-11-28, 2:58 |
| 2014-11-28, 3:19 | 2014-11-28, 3:27 |
| 2014-11-28, 3:48 | 2014-11-28, 3:56 |
| 2014-11-28, 4:18 | 2014-11-28, 4:25 |
| 2014-11-28, 4:47 | 2014-11-28, 4:55 |
| 2014-11-28, 5:16 | 2014-11-28, 5:24 |
| 2014-11-28, 5:45 | 2014-11-28, 5:54 |
| 2014-11-28, 6:15 | 2014-11-28, 6:23 |
| 2014-11-28, 6:44 | 2014-11-28, 6:53 |
| 2014-11-28, 7:14 | 2014-11-28, 7:22 |
| 2014-11-28, 7:43 | 2014-11-28, 7:51 |
| 2014-11-28, 8:13 | 2014-11-28, 8:21 |
| 2014-11-28, 8:42 | 2014-11-28, 8:50 |
| 2014-11-28, 9:12 | 2014-11-28, 9:20 |
| 2014-11-28, 9:42 | 2014-11-28, 9:50 |
| 2014-11-28, 10:11 | 2014-11-28, 10:19 |
| 2014-11-28, 10:41 | 2014-11-28, 10:48 |
| 2014-11-28, 11:10 | 2014-11-28, 11:18 |
| 2014-11-28, 11:39 | 2014-11-28, 11:47 |
| 2014-11-28, 12: 9 | 2014-11-28, 12:17 |
| 2014-11-28, 12:38 | 2014-11-28, 12:46 |
| 2014-11-28, 13: 7 | 2014-11-28, 13:15 |
| 2014-11-28, 13:36 | 2014-11-28, 13:44 |
| 2014-11-28, 14: 6 | 2014-11-28, 14:14 |
| 2014-11-28, 14:35 | 2014-11-28, 14:43 |
| 2014-11-28, 15: 4 | 2014-11-28, 15:12 |
| 2014-11-28, 15:34 | 2014-11-28, 15:42 |
| 2014-11-28, 16: 3 | 2014-11-28, 16:11 |
| 2014-11-28, 16:32 | 2014-11-28, 16:40 |
| 2014-11-28, 17: 1 | 2014-11-28, 17: 9 |
| 2014-11-28, 17:30 | 2014-11-28, 17:38 |
| 2014-11-28, 18: 0 | 2014-11-28, 18: 8 |
| 2014-11-28, 18:29 | 2014-11-28, 18:37 |
| 2014-11-28, 18:58 | 2014-11-28, 19: 6 |
| 2014-11-28, 19:27 | 2014-11-28, 19:35 |
| 2014-11-28, 19:56 | 2014-11-28, 20: 4 |
| 2014-11-28, 20:26 | 2014-11-28, 20:34 |
| 2014-11-28, 20:55 | 2014-11-28, 21: 3 |
| 2014-11-28, 21:24 | 2014-11-28, 21:32 |
| 2014-11-28, 21:53 | 2014-11-28, 22: 1 |
| 2014-11-28, 22:22 | 2014-11-28, 22:30 |
| 2014-11-28, 22:52 | 2014-11-28, 23: 0 |
| 2014-11-28, 23:21 | 2014-11-28, 23:29 |
| 2014-11-28, 23:50 | 2014-11-28, 23:58 |
| 2014-11-29, 0:20 | 2014-11-29, 0:28 |
| 2014-11-29, 0:49 | 2014-11-29, 0:57 |
| 2014-11-29, 1:19 | 2014-11-29, 1:27 |
| 2014-11-29, 1:49 | 2014-11-29, 1:57 |
| 2014-11-29, 2:18 | 2014-11-29, 2:26 |
| 2014-11-29, 2:48 | 2014-11-29, 2:56 |
| 2014-11-29, 3:17 | 2014-11-29, 3:25 |
| 2014-11-29, 3:47 | 2014-11-29, 3:55 |
| 2014-11-29, 4:17 | 2014-11-29, 4:25 |
| 2014-11-29, 4:47 | 2014-11-29, 4:55 |
| 2014-11-29, 5:17 | 2014-11-29, 5:25 |
| 2014-11-29, 5:47 | 2014-11-29, 5:55 |
| 2014-11-29, 6:17 | 2014-11-29, 6:25 |
| 2014-11-29, 6:46 | 2014-11-29, 6:54 |
| 2014-11-29, 7:16 | 2014-11-29, 7:24 |
| 2014-11-29, 7:45 | 2014-11-29, 7:53 |
| 2014-11-29, 8:15 | 2014-11-29, 8:23 |
| 2014-11-29, 8:44 | 2014-11-29, 8:52 |
| 2014-11-29, 9:14 | 2014-11-29, 9:22 |
| 2014-11-29, 9:44 | 2014-11-29, 9:52 |
| 2014-11-29, 10:14 | 2014-11-29, 10:21 |
| 2014-11-29, 10:43 | 2014-11-29, 10:51 |
| 2014-11-29, 11:13 | 2014-11-29, 11:20 |
| 2014-11-29, 11:42 | 2014-11-29, 11:50 |
| 2014-11-29, 12:11 | 2014-11-29, 12:19 |
| 2014-11-29, 12:40 | 2014-11-29, 12:48 |
| 2014-11-29, 13:10 | 2014-11-29, 13:18 |
| 2014-11-29, 13:39 | 2014-11-29, 13:47 |
| 2014-11-29, 14: 8 | 2014-11-29, 14:16 |
| 2014-11-29, 14:38 | 2014-11-29, 14:46 |
| 2014-11-29, 15: 7 | 2014-11-29, 15:15 |
| 2014-11-29, 15:36 | 2014-11-29, 15:44 |
| 2014-11-29, 16: 5 | 2014-11-29, 16:13 |
| 2014-11-29, 16:35 | 2014-11-29, 16:42 |
| 2014-11-29, 17: 4 | 2014-11-29, 17:12 |
| 2014-11-29, 17:33 | 2014-11-29, 17:41 |
| 2014-11-29, 18: 3 | 2014-11-29, 18:11 |
| 2014-11-29, 18:32 | 2014-11-29, 18:40 |
| 2014-11-29, 19: 2 | 2014-11-29, 19:10 |
| 2014-11-29, 19:31 | 2014-11-29, 19:39 |
| 2014-11-29, 20: 1 | 2014-11-29, 20: 8 |
| 2014-11-29, 20:30 | 2014-11-29, 20:38 |
| 2014-11-29, 20:59 | 2014-11-29, 21: 7 |
| 2014-11-29, 21:29 | 2014-11-29, 21:37 |
| 2014-11-29, 21:59 | 2014-11-29, 22: 7 |
| 2014-11-29, 22:29 | 2014-11-29, 22:37 |
| 2014-11-29, 22:58 | 2014-11-29, 23: 6 |
| 2014-11-29, 23:28 | 2014-11-29, 23:36 |
| 2014-11-29, 23:58 | 2014-11-30, 0: 6 |
| 2014-11-30, 0:28 | 2014-11-30, 0:35 |
| 2014-11-30, 0:57 | 2014-11-30, 1: 5 |
| 2014-11-30, 1:27 | 2014-11-30, 1:35 |
| 2014-11-30, 1:56 | 2014-11-30, 2: 4 |
| 2014-11-30, 2:26 | 2014-11-30, 2:33 |
| 2014-11-30, 2:55 | 2014-11-30, 3: 3 |
| 2014-11-30, 3:24 | 2014-11-30, 3:32 |
| 2014-11-30, 3:54 | 2014-11-30, 4: 2 |
| 2014-11-30, 4:23 | 2014-11-30, 4:31 |
| 2014-11-30, 4:53 | 2014-11-30, 5: 0 |
| 2014-11-30, 5:23 | 2014-11-30, 5:31 |
| 2014-11-30, 5:53 | 2014-11-30, 6: 1 |
| 2014-11-30, 6:23 | 2014-11-30, 6:31 |
| 2014-11-30, 6:52 | 2014-11-30, 7: 0 |
| 2014-11-30, 7:22 | 2014-11-30, 7:30 |
| 2014-11-30, 7:52 | 2014-11-30, 8: 0 |
| 2014-11-30, 8:22 | 2014-11-30, 8:30 |
| 2014-11-30, 8:48 | 2014-11-30, 8:56 |
| 2014-11-30, 9:15 | 2014-11-30, 9:22 |
| 2014-11-30, 9:42 | 2014-11-30, 9:51 |
| 2014-11-30, 10: 7 | 2014-11-30, 10:15 |
| 2014-11-30, 10:34 | 2014-11-30, 10:42 |
| 2014-11-30, 11: 2 | 2014-11-30, 11:10 |
| 2014-11-30, 11:30 | 2014-11-30, 11:38 |
| 2014-11-30, 11:59 | 2014-11-30, 12: 6 |
| 2014-11-30, 12:27 | 2014-11-30, 12:35 |
| 2014-11-30, 12:57 | 2014-11-30, 13: 5 |
| 2014-11-30, 13:27 | 2014-11-30, 13:36 |
| 2014-11-30, 13:53 | 2014-11-30, 14: 1 |
| 2014-11-30, 14:20 | 2014-11-30, 14:29 |
| 2014-11-30, 14:45 | 2014-11-30, 14:53 |
| 2014-11-30, 15:12 | 2014-11-30, 15:20 |
| 2014-11-30, 15:39 | 2014-11-30, 15:47 |

```
2014-11-30, 16: 8 | 2014-11-30, 16:15      2014-12- 2, 1:24 | 2014-12- 2, 1:32      2014-12- 3, 9:30 | 2014-12- 3, 9:38
2014-11-30, 16:36 | 2014-11-30, 16:44      2014-12- 2, 1:54 | 2014-12- 2, 2: 2      2014-12- 3, 10: 0 | 2014-12- 3, 10: 7
2014-11-30, 17: 0 | 2014-11-30, 17: 9      2014-12- 2, 2:24 | 2014-12- 2, 2:32      2014-12- 3, 10:29 | 2014-12- 3, 10:37
2014-11-30, 17:23 | 2014-11-30, 17:30      2014-12- 2, 2:55 | 2014-12- 2, 3: 3      2014-12- 3, 10:59 | 2014-12- 3, 11: 7
2014-11-30, 17:46 | 2014-11-30, 17:53      2014-12- 2, 3:25 | 2014-12- 2, 3:33      2014-12- 3, 11:29 | 2014-12- 3, 11:37
2014-11-30, 18:13 | 2014-11-30, 18:20      2014-12- 2, 3:55 | 2014-12- 2, 4: 3      2014-12- 3, 11:59 | 2014-12- 3, 12: 6
2014-11-30, 18:41 | 2014-11-30, 18:48      2014-12- 2, 4:25 | 2014-12- 2, 4:33      2014-12- 3, 12:28 | 2014-12- 3, 12:37
2014-11-30, 19: 9 | 2014-11-30, 19:17      2014-12- 2, 4:55 | 2014-12- 2, 5: 2      2014-12- 3, 12:58 | 2014-12- 3, 13: 6
2014-11-30, 19:38 | 2014-11-30, 19:45      2014-12- 2, 5:24 | 2014-12- 2, 5:32      2014-12- 3, 13:28 | 2014-12- 3, 13:35
2014-11-30, 20: 7 | 2014-11-30, 20:14      2014-12- 2, 5:53 | 2014-12- 2, 6: 1      2014-12- 3, 13:57 | 2014-12- 3, 14: 5
2014-11-30, 20:35 | 2014-11-30, 20:43      2014-12- 2, 6:23 | 2014-12- 2, 6:31      2014-12- 3, 14:27 | 2014-12- 3, 14:34
2014-11-30, 21: 4 | 2014-11-30, 21:12      2014-12- 2, 6:53 | 2014-12- 2, 7: 1      2014-12- 3, 14:56 | 2014-12- 3, 15: 4
2014-11-30, 21:33 | 2014-11-30, 21:41      2014-12- 2, 7:23 | 2014-12- 2, 7:31      2014-12- 3, 15:26 | 2014-12- 3, 15:34
2014-11-30, 22: 2 | 2014-11-30, 22:10      2014-12- 2, 7:53 | 2014-12- 2, 8: 1      2014-12- 3, 15:55 | 2014-12- 3, 16: 3
2014-11-30, 22:31 | 2014-11-30, 22:39      2014-12- 2, 8:22 | 2014-12- 2, 8:31      2014-12- 3, 16:25 | 2014-12- 3, 16:32
2014-11-30, 23: 1 | 2014-11-30, 23: 9      2014-12- 2, 8:46 | 2014-12- 2, 8:54      2014-12- 3, 16:54 | 2014-12- 3, 17: 1
2014-11-30, 23:30 | 2014-11-30, 23:38      2014-12- 2, 9:10 | 2014-12- 2, 9:17      2014-12- 3, 17:23 | 2014-12- 3, 17:31
2014-11-30, 23:59 | 2014-12- 1, 0: 7       2014-12- 2, 9:34 | 2014-12- 2, 9:42      2014-12- 3, 17:52 | 2014-12- 3, 18: 0
2014-12- 1, 0:28 | 2014-12- 1, 0:36        2014-12- 2, 9:59 | 2014-12- 2, 10: 6     2014-12- 3, 18:21 | 2014-12- 3, 18:29
2014-12- 1, 0:58 | 2014-12- 1, 1: 6        2014-12- 2, 10:24 | 2014-12- 2, 10:32    2014-12- 3, 18:50 | 2014-12- 3, 18:58
2014-12- 1, 1:27 | 2014-12- 1, 1:35        2014-12- 2, 10:50 | 2014-12- 2, 10:58    2014-12- 3, 19:20 | 2014-12- 3, 19:28
2014-12- 1, 1:57 | 2014-12- 1, 2: 5        2014-12- 2, 11:16 | 2014-12- 2, 11:24    2014-12- 3, 19:49 | 2014-12- 3, 19:57
2014-12- 1, 2:27 | 2014-12- 1, 2:35        2014-12- 2, 11:43 | 2014-12- 2, 11:51    2014-12- 3, 20:19 | 2014-12- 3, 20:27
2014-12- 1, 2:57 | 2014-12- 1, 3: 5        2014-12- 2, 12:10 | 2014-12- 2, 12:18    2014-12- 3, 20:48 | 2014-12- 3, 20:56
2014-12- 1, 3:26 | 2014-12- 1, 3:34        2014-12- 2, 12:37 | 2014-12- 2, 12:44    2014-12- 3, 21:18 | 2014-12- 3, 21:26
2014-12- 1, 3:56 | 2014-12- 1, 4: 4        2014-12- 2, 13: 4 | 2014-12- 2, 13:12    2014-12- 3, 21:47 | 2014-12- 3, 21:55
2014-12- 1, 4:25 | 2014-12- 1, 4:33        2014-12- 2, 13:31 | 2014-12- 2, 13:38    2014-12- 3, 22:17 | 2014-12- 3, 22:25
2014-12- 1, 4:55 | 2014-12- 1, 5: 3        2014-12- 2, 13:58 | 2014-12- 2, 14: 6    2014-12- 3, 22:47 | 2014-12- 3, 22:55
2014-12- 1, 5:25 | 2014-12- 1, 5:33        2014-12- 2, 14:25 | 2014-12- 2, 14:33    2014-12- 3, 23:16 | 2014-12- 3, 23:25
2014-12- 1, 5:55 | 2014-12- 1, 6: 3        2014-12- 2, 14:52 | 2014-12- 2, 15: 0    2014-12- 3, 23:47 | 2014-12- 3, 23:55
2014-12- 1, 6:25 | 2014-12- 1, 6:33        2014-12- 2, 15:20 | 2014-12- 2, 15:27    2014-12- 4, 0:16 | 2014-12- 4, 0:25
2014-12- 1, 6:56 | 2014-12- 1, 7: 4        2014-12- 2, 15:47 | 2014-12- 2, 15:54    2014-12- 4, 0:47 | 2014-12- 4, 0:55
2014-12- 1, 7:26 | 2014-12- 1, 7:34        2014-12- 2, 16:14 | 2014-12- 2, 16:21    2014-12- 4, 1:17 | 2014-12- 4, 1:25
2014-12- 1, 7:57 | 2014-12- 1, 8: 5        2014-12- 2, 16:41 | 2014-12- 2, 16:49    2014-12- 4, 1:47 | 2014-12- 4, 1:54
2014-12- 1, 8:27 | 2014-12- 1, 8:35        2014-12- 2, 17: 8 | 2014-12- 2, 17:16    2014-12- 4, 2:16 | 2014-12- 4, 2:24
2014-12- 1, 8:57 | 2014-12- 1, 9: 5        2014-12- 2, 17:36 | 2014-12- 2, 17:44    2014-12- 4, 2:46 | 2014-12- 4, 2:54
2014-12- 1, 9:27 | 2014-12- 1, 9:35        2014-12- 2, 18: 4 | 2014-12- 2, 18:12    2014-12- 4, 3:16 | 2014-12- 4, 3:24
2014-12- 1, 9:57 | 2014-12- 1, 10: 5       2014-12- 2, 18:32 | 2014-12- 2, 18:40    2014-12- 4, 3:45 | 2014-12- 4, 3:53
2014-12- 1, 10:26 | 2014-12- 1, 10:35      2014-12- 2, 19: 1 | 2014-12- 2, 19: 9    2014-12- 4, 4:15 | 2014-12- 4, 4:23
2014-12- 1, 10:56 | 2014-12- 1, 11: 4      2014-12- 2, 19:30 | 2014-12- 2, 19:38    2014-12- 4, 4:45 | 2014-12- 4, 4:53
2014-12- 1, 11:27 | 2014-12- 1, 11:35      2014-12- 2, 19:58 | 2014-12- 2, 20: 6    2014-12- 4, 5:16 | 2014-12- 4, 5:24
2014-12- 1, 11:57 | 2014-12- 1, 12: 5      2014-12- 2, 20:27 | 2014-12- 2, 20:34    2014-12- 4, 5:46 | 2014-12- 4, 5:54
2014-12- 1, 12:27 | 2014-12- 1, 12:35      2014-12- 2, 20:52 | 2014-12- 2, 21: 0    2014-12- 4, 6:16 | 2014-12- 4, 6:23
2014-12- 1, 12:57 | 2014-12- 1, 13: 5      2014-12- 2, 21:19 | 2014-12- 2, 21:27    2014-12- 4, 6:45 | 2014-12- 4, 6:53
2014-12- 1, 13:27 | 2014-12- 1, 13:35      2014-12- 2, 21:47 | 2014-12- 2, 21:55    2014-12- 4, 7:15 | 2014-12- 4, 7:22
2014-12- 1, 13:57 | 2014-12- 1, 14: 4      2014-12- 2, 22:15 | 2014-12- 2, 22:23    2014-12- 4, 7:44 | 2014-12- 4, 7:52
2014-12- 1, 14:26 | 2014-12- 1, 14:34      2014-12- 2, 22:44 | 2014-12- 2, 22:52    2014-12- 4, 8:14 | 2014-12- 4, 8:22
2014-12- 1, 14:57 | 2014-12- 1, 15: 5      2014-12- 2, 23:12 | 2014-12- 2, 23:20    2014-12- 4, 8:44 | 2014-12- 4, 8:51
2014-12- 1, 15:27 | 2014-12- 1, 15:35      2014-12- 2, 23:41 | 2014-12- 2, 23:49    2014-12- 4, 9:13 | 2014-12- 4, 9:21
2014-12- 1, 15:57 | 2014-12- 1, 16: 5      2014-12- 3, 0:10 | 2014-12- 3, 0:18      2014-12- 4, 9:43 | 2014-12- 4, 9:50
2014-12- 1, 16:27 | 2014-12- 1, 16:35      2014-12- 3, 0:40 | 2014-12- 3, 0:48      2014-12- 4, 10:12 | 2014-12- 4, 10:20
2014-12- 1, 16:57 | 2014-12- 1, 17: 5      2014-12- 3, 1: 9 | 2014-12- 3, 1:17      2014-12- 4, 10:42 | 2014-12- 4, 10:50
2014-12- 1, 17:27 | 2014-12- 1, 17:35      2014-12- 3, 1:38 | 2014-12- 3, 1:46      2014-12- 4, 11:12 | 2014-12- 4, 11:19
2014-12- 1, 17:57 | 2014-12- 1, 18: 5      2014-12- 3, 2: 7 | 2014-12- 3, 2:15      2014-12- 4, 11:41 | 2014-12- 4, 11:49
2014-12- 1, 18:27 | 2014-12- 1, 18:34      2014-12- 3, 2:37 | 2014-12- 3, 2:44      2014-12- 4, 12:11 | 2014-12- 4, 12:18
2014-12- 1, 18:56 | 2014-12- 1, 19: 4      2014-12- 3, 3: 6 | 2014-12- 3, 3:14      2014-12- 4, 12:40 | 2014-12- 4, 12:48
2014-12- 1, 19:26 | 2014-12- 1, 19:34      2014-12- 3, 3:35 | 2014-12- 3, 3:43      2014-12- 4, 13:10 | 2014-12- 4, 13:18
2014-12- 1, 19:55 | 2014-12- 1, 20: 3      2014-12- 3, 4: 5 | 2014-12- 3, 4:13      2014-12- 4, 13:39 | 2014-12- 4, 13:47
2014-12- 1, 20:25 | 2014-12- 1, 20:33      2014-12- 3, 4:34 | 2014-12- 3, 4:42      2014-12- 4, 14: 9 | 2014-12- 4, 14:17
2014-12- 1, 20:55 | 2014-12- 1, 21: 3      2014-12- 3, 5: 4 | 2014-12- 3, 5:12      2014-12- 4, 14:38 | 2014-12- 4, 14:46
2014-12- 1, 21:25 | 2014-12- 1, 21:33      2014-12- 3, 5:34 | 2014-12- 3, 5:41      2014-12- 4, 15: 8 | 2014-12- 4, 15:16
2014-12- 1, 21:55 | 2014-12- 1, 22: 3      2014-12- 3, 6: 3 | 2014-12- 3, 6:11      2014-12- 4, 15:38 | 2014-12- 4, 15:46
2014-12- 1, 22:25 | 2014-12- 1, 22:33      2014-12- 3, 6:33 | 2014-12- 3, 6:40      2014-12- 4, 16: 8 | 2014-12- 4, 16:16
2014-12- 1, 22:55 | 2014-12- 1, 23: 3      2014-12- 3, 7: 2 | 2014-12- 3, 7:10      2014-12- 4, 16:37 | 2014-12- 4, 16:45
2014-12- 1, 23:25 | 2014-12- 1, 23:33      2014-12- 3, 7:31 | 2014-12- 3, 7:39      2014-12- 4, 17: 7 | 2014-12- 4, 17:14
2014-12- 1, 23:55 | 2014-12- 2, 0: 3       2014-12- 3, 8: 1 | 2014-12- 3, 8: 9      2014-12- 4, 17:36 | 2014-12- 4, 17:44
2014-12- 2, 0:25 | 2014-12- 2, 0:32        2014-12- 3, 8:31 | 2014-12- 3, 8:39      2014-12- 4, 18: 6 | 2014-12- 4, 18:13
2014-12- 2, 0:54 | 2014-12- 2, 1: 2        2014-12- 3, 9: 1 | 2014-12- 3, 9: 8      2014-12- 4, 18:35 | 2014-12- 4, 18:42
```

```
2014-12- 4, 19: 3 | 2014-12- 4, 19:12      2014-12- 6, 3:14 | 2014-12- 6, 3:21      2014-12- 7, 8:29 | 2014-12- 7, 8:36
2014-12- 4, 19:31 | 2014-12- 4, 19:39      2014-12- 6, 3:43 | 2014-12- 6, 3:51      2014-12- 7, 8:54 | 2014-12- 7, 9: 2
2014-12- 4, 20: 0 | 2014-12- 4, 20: 7      2014-12- 6, 4:13 | 2014-12- 6, 4:20      2014-12- 7, 9:20 | 2014-12- 7, 9:27
2014-12- 4, 20:28 | 2014-12- 4, 20:36      2014-12- 6, 4:42 | 2014-12- 6, 4:50      2014-12- 7, 9:46 | 2014-12- 7, 9:53
2014-12- 4, 20:57 | 2014-12- 4, 21: 5      2014-12- 6, 5:11 | 2014-12- 6, 5:19      2014-12- 7, 10:12 | 2014-12- 7, 10:19
2014-12- 4, 21:26 | 2014-12- 4, 21:34      2014-12- 6, 5:41 | 2014-12- 6, 5:48      2014-12- 7, 10:38 | 2014-12- 7, 10:45
2014-12- 4, 21:56 | 2014-12- 4, 22: 4      2014-12- 6, 6:10 | 2014-12- 6, 6:18      2014-12- 7, 11: 4 | 2014-12- 7, 11:13
2014-12- 4, 22:27 | 2014-12- 4, 22:34      2014-12- 6, 6:39 | 2014-12- 6, 6:47      2014-12- 7, 11:28 | 2014-12- 7, 11:35
2014-12- 4, 22:56 | 2014-12- 4, 23: 4      2014-12- 6, 7: 9 | 2014-12- 6, 7:16      2014-12- 7, 11:53 | 2014-12- 7, 12: 0
2014-12- 4, 23:26 | 2014-12- 4, 23:34      2014-12- 6, 7:38 | 2014-12- 6, 7:45      2014-12- 7, 12:18 | 2014-12- 7, 12:26
2014-12- 4, 23:56 | 2014-12- 5, 0: 4      2014-12- 6, 8: 7 | 2014-12- 6, 8:15      2014-12- 7, 12:44 | 2014-12- 7, 12:51
2014-12- 5, 0:26 | 2014-12- 5, 0:33      2014-12- 6, 8:36 | 2014-12- 6, 8:44      2014-12- 7, 13:10 | 2014-12- 7, 13:17
2014-12- 5, 0:55 | 2014-12- 5, 1: 3      2014-12- 6, 9: 5 | 2014-12- 6, 9:13      2014-12- 7, 13:36 | 2014-12- 7, 13:43
2014-12- 5, 1:25 | 2014-12- 5, 1:32      2014-12- 6, 9:30 | 2014-12- 6, 9:37      2014-12- 7, 14: 3 | 2014-12- 7, 14:10
2014-12- 5, 1:54 | 2014-12- 5, 2: 2      2014-12- 6, 9:57 | 2014-12- 6, 10: 5      2014-12- 7, 14:29 | 2014-12- 7, 14:36
2014-12- 5, 2:24 | 2014-12- 5, 2:32      2014-12- 6, 10:26 | 2014-12- 6, 10:34      2014-12- 7, 14:56 | 2014-12- 7, 15: 3
2014-12- 5, 2:53 | 2014-12- 5, 3: 1      2014-12- 6, 10:55 | 2014-12- 6, 11: 2      2014-12- 7, 15:23 | 2014-12- 7, 15:30
2014-12- 5, 3:23 | 2014-12- 5, 3:31      2014-12- 6, 11:23 | 2014-12- 6, 11:31      2014-12- 7, 15:50 | 2014-12- 7, 15:58
2014-12- 5, 3:52 | 2014-12- 5, 4: 0      2014-12- 6, 11:52 | 2014-12- 6, 12: 0      2014-12- 7, 16:17 | 2014-12- 7, 16:24
2014-12- 5, 4:22 | 2014-12- 5, 4:30      2014-12- 6, 12:21 | 2014-12- 6, 12:28      2014-12- 7, 16:44 | 2014-12- 7, 16:51
2014-12- 5, 4:51 | 2014-12- 5, 4:59      2014-12- 6, 12:49 | 2014-12- 6, 12:57      2014-12- 7, 17:11 | 2014-12- 7, 17:18
2014-12- 5, 5:21 | 2014-12- 5, 5:29      2014-12- 6, 13:18 | 2014-12- 6, 13:26      2014-12- 7, 17:39 | 2014-12- 7, 17:46
2014-12- 5, 5:50 | 2014-12- 5, 5:58      2014-12- 6, 13:47 | 2014-12- 6, 13:54      2014-12- 7, 18: 6 | 2014-12- 7, 18:14
2014-12- 5, 6:20 | 2014-12- 5, 6:28      2014-12- 6, 14:15 | 2014-12- 6, 14:23      2014-12- 7, 18:33 | 2014-12- 7, 18:41
2014-12- 5, 6:50 | 2014-12- 5, 6:57      2014-12- 6, 14:44 | 2014-12- 6, 14:52      2014-12- 7, 19: 1 | 2014-12- 7, 19: 8
2014-12- 5, 7:18 | 2014-12- 5, 7:27      2014-12- 6, 15:13 | 2014-12- 6, 15:21      2014-12- 7, 19:28 | 2014-12- 7, 19:35
2014-12- 5, 7:45 | 2014-12- 5, 7:53      2014-12- 6, 15:42 | 2014-12- 6, 15:50      2014-12- 7, 19:55 | 2014-12- 7, 20: 3
2014-12- 5, 8:10 | 2014-12- 5, 8:19      2014-12- 6, 16:11 | 2014-12- 6, 16:19      2014-12- 7, 20:23 | 2014-12- 7, 20:30
2014-12- 5, 8:33 | 2014-12- 5, 8:40      2014-12- 6, 16:41 | 2014-12- 6, 16:48      2014-12- 7, 20:50 | 2014-12- 7, 20:58
2014-12- 5, 8:57 | 2014-12- 5, 9: 4      2014-12- 6, 17: 9 | 2014-12- 6, 17:17      2014-12- 7, 21:18 | 2014-12- 7, 21:25
2014-12- 5, 9:22 | 2014-12- 5, 9:29      2014-12- 6, 17:33 | 2014-12- 6, 17:41      2014-12- 7, 21:45 | 2014-12- 7, 21:53
2014-12- 5, 9:47 | 2014-12- 5, 9:54      2014-12- 6, 17:57 | 2014-12- 6, 18: 4      2014-12- 7, 22:13 | 2014-12- 7, 22:20
2014-12- 5, 10:13 | 2014-12- 5, 10:20      2014-12- 6, 18:20 | 2014-12- 6, 18:28      2014-12- 7, 22:41 | 2014-12- 7, 22:48
2014-12- 5, 10:39 | 2014-12- 5, 10:46      2014-12- 6, 18:43 | 2014-12- 6, 18:51      2014-12- 7, 23: 8 | 2014-12- 7, 23:16
2014-12- 5, 11: 5 | 2014-12- 5, 11:13      2014-12- 6, 19: 7 | 2014-12- 6, 19:14      2014-12- 7, 23:36 | 2014-12- 7, 23:44
2014-12- 5, 11:32 | 2014-12- 5, 11:40      2014-12- 6, 19:30 | 2014-12- 6, 19:37      2014-12- 8, 0: 4 | 2014-12- 8, 0:11
2014-12- 5, 11:59 | 2014-12- 5, 12: 7      2014-12- 6, 19:53 | 2014-12- 6, 20: 0      2014-12- 8, 0:31 | 2014-12- 8, 0:39
2014-12- 5, 12:27 | 2014-12- 5, 12:34      2014-12- 6, 20:16 | 2014-12- 6, 20:23      2014-12- 8, 0:59 | 2014-12- 8, 1: 7
2014-12- 5, 12:54 | 2014-12- 5, 13: 2      2014-12- 6, 20:39 | 2014-12- 6, 20:47      2014-12- 8, 1:27 | 2014-12- 8, 1:35
2014-12- 5, 13:22 | 2014-12- 5, 13:29      2014-12- 6, 21: 2 | 2014-12- 6, 21:10      2014-12- 8, 1:55 | 2014-12- 8, 2: 3
2014-12- 5, 13:50 | 2014-12- 5, 13:57      2014-12- 6, 21:25 | 2014-12- 6, 21:33      2014-12- 8, 2:23 | 2014-12- 8, 2:31
2014-12- 5, 14:18 | 2014-12- 5, 14:25      2014-12- 6, 21:48 | 2014-12- 6, 21:56      2014-12- 8, 2:52 | 2014-12- 8, 2:59
2014-12- 5, 14:45 | 2014-12- 5, 14:53      2014-12- 6, 22:11 | 2014-12- 6, 22:19      2014-12- 8, 3:20 | 2014-12- 8, 3:27
2014-12- 5, 15:14 | 2014-12- 5, 15:21      2014-12- 6, 22:34 | 2014-12- 6, 22:42      2014-12- 8, 3:48 | 2014-12- 8, 3:55
2014-12- 5, 15:42 | 2014-12- 5, 15:49      2014-12- 6, 22:57 | 2014-12- 6, 23: 4      2014-12- 8, 4:16 | 2014-12- 8, 4:23
2014-12- 5, 16:10 | 2014-12- 5, 16:18      2014-12- 6, 23:20 | 2014-12- 6, 23:27      2014-12- 8, 4:44 | 2014-12- 8, 4:51
2014-12- 5, 16:39 | 2014-12- 5, 16:46      2014-12- 6, 23:43 | 2014-12- 6, 23:51      2014-12- 8, 5:12 | 2014-12- 8, 5:19
2014-12- 5, 17: 7 | 2014-12- 5, 17:15      2014-12- 7, 0: 6 | 2014-12- 7, 0:14      2014-12- 8, 5:40 | 2014-12- 8, 5:47
2014-12- 5, 17:36 | 2014-12- 5, 17:43      2014-12- 7, 0:30 | 2014-12- 7, 0:37      2014-12- 8, 6: 8 | 2014-12- 8, 6:15
2014-12- 5, 18: 4 | 2014-12- 5, 18:12      2014-12- 7, 0:53 | 2014-12- 7, 1: 0      2014-12- 8, 6:36 | 2014-12- 8, 6:43
2014-12- 5, 18:33 | 2014-12- 5, 18:40      2014-12- 7, 1:16 | 2014-12- 7, 1:23      2014-12- 8, 7: 4 | 2014-12- 8, 7:12
2014-12- 5, 19: 1 | 2014-12- 5, 19: 9      2014-12- 7, 1:39 | 2014-12- 7, 1:47      2014-12- 8, 7:33 | 2014-12- 8, 7:40
2014-12- 5, 19:30 | 2014-12- 5, 19:37      2014-12- 7, 2: 3 | 2014-12- 7, 2:10      2014-12- 8, 8: 1 | 2014-12- 8, 8: 8
2014-12- 5, 19:59 | 2014-12- 5, 20: 6      2014-12- 7, 2:26 | 2014-12- 7, 2:33      2014-12- 8, 8:29 | 2014-12- 8, 8:37
2014-12- 5, 20:28 | 2014-12- 5, 20:35      2014-12- 7, 2:49 | 2014-12- 7, 2:57      2014-12- 8, 8:58 | 2014-12- 8, 9: 5
2014-12- 5, 20:57 | 2014-12- 5, 21: 4      2014-12- 7, 3:13 | 2014-12- 7, 3:21      2014-12- 8, 9:27 | 2014-12- 8, 9:34
2014-12- 5, 21:25 | 2014-12- 5, 21:33      2014-12- 7, 3:37 | 2014-12- 7, 3:44      2014-12- 8, 9:55 | 2014-12- 8, 10: 2
2014-12- 5, 21:54 | 2014-12- 5, 22: 2      2014-12- 7, 4: 1 | 2014-12- 7, 4: 8      2014-12- 8, 10:23 | 2014-12- 8, 10:31
2014-12- 5, 22:23 | 2014-12- 5, 22:31      2014-12- 7, 4:24 | 2014-12- 7, 4:31      2014-12- 8, 10:52 | 2014-12- 8, 10:59
2014-12- 5, 22:53 | 2014-12- 5, 23: 0      2014-12- 7, 4:48 | 2014-12- 7, 4:55      2014-12- 8, 11:20 | 2014-12- 8, 11:27
2014-12- 5, 23:22 | 2014-12- 5, 23:29      2014-12- 7, 5:12 | 2014-12- 7, 5:19      2014-12- 8, 11:48 | 2014-12- 8, 11:56
2014-12- 5, 23:50 | 2014-12- 5, 23:58      2014-12- 7, 5:36 | 2014-12- 7, 5:44      2014-12- 8, 12:16 | 2014-12- 8, 12:24
2014-12- 6, 0:19 | 2014-12- 6, 0:27      2014-12- 7, 6: 1 | 2014-12- 7, 6: 8      2014-12- 8, 12:45 | 2014-12- 8, 12:53
2014-12- 6, 0:48 | 2014-12- 6, 0:56      2014-12- 7, 6:25 | 2014-12- 7, 6:32      2014-12- 8, 13:14 | 2014-12- 8, 13:21
2014-12- 6, 1:17 | 2014-12- 6, 1:24      2014-12- 7, 6:49 | 2014-12- 7, 6:56      2014-12- 8, 13:42 | 2014-12- 8, 13:50
2014-12- 6, 1:46 | 2014-12- 6, 1:54      2014-12- 7, 7:14 | 2014-12- 7, 7:21      2014-12- 8, 14:11 | 2014-12- 8, 14:18
2014-12- 6, 2:15 | 2014-12- 6, 2:23      2014-12- 7, 7:39 | 2014-12- 7, 7:46      2014-12- 8, 14:39 | 2014-12- 8, 14:47
2014-12- 6, 2:44 | 2014-12- 6, 2:52      2014-12- 7, 8: 4 | 2014-12- 7, 8:11      2014-12- 8, 15: 8 | 2014-12- 8, 15:16
```

```
2014-12- 8, 15:37 | 2014-12- 8, 15:45      2014-12- 9, 21: 1 | 2014-12- 9, 21: 8      2014-12-11, 14: 2 | 2014-12-11, 14:10
2014-12- 8, 16: 6 | 2014-12- 8, 16:13      2014-12- 9, 21:30 | 2014-12- 9, 21:37      2014-12-11, 14:25 | 2014-12-11, 14:33
2014-12- 8, 16:34 | 2014-12- 8, 16:42      2014-12- 9, 21:59 | 2014-12- 9, 22: 7      2014-12-11, 14:50 | 2014-12-11, 14:57
2014-12- 8, 17: 2 | 2014-12- 8, 17:10      2014-12- 9, 22:29 | 2014-12- 9, 22:36      2014-12-11, 15:14 | 2014-12-11, 15:22
2014-12- 8, 17:31 | 2014-12- 8, 17:39      2014-12- 9, 22:58 | 2014-12- 9, 23: 5      2014-12-11, 15:39 | 2014-12-11, 15:47
2014-12- 8, 18: 0 | 2014-12- 8, 18: 7      2014-12- 9, 23:27 | 2014-12- 9, 23:34      2014-12-11, 16: 4 | 2014-12-11, 16:12
2014-12- 8, 18:29 | 2014-12- 8, 18:36      2014-12-10, 8:38 | 2014-12-10, 8:45        2014-12-11, 16:30 | 2014-12-11, 16:37
2014-12- 8, 18:57 | 2014-12- 8, 19: 5      2014-12-10, 9: 1 | 2014-12-10, 9: 8        2014-12-11, 16:56 | 2014-12-11, 17: 3
2014-12- 8, 19:26 | 2014-12- 8, 19:34      2014-12-10, 9:27 | 2014-12-10, 9:34        2014-12-11, 17:21 | 2014-12-11, 17:28
2014-12- 8, 19:55 | 2014-12- 8, 20: 3      2014-12-10, 9:55 | 2014-12-10, 10: 2       2014-12-11, 17:47 | 2014-12-11, 17:54
2014-12- 8, 20:23 | 2014-12- 8, 20:32      2014-12-10, 10:23 | 2014-12-10, 10:30      2014-12-11, 18:12 | 2014-12-11, 18:20
2014-12- 8, 20:46 | 2014-12- 8, 20:53      2014-12-10, 10:51 | 2014-12-10, 10:58      2014-12-11, 18:38 | 2014-12-11, 18:45
2014-12- 8, 21: 8 | 2014-12- 8, 21:15      2014-12-10, 11:19 | 2014-12-10, 11:26      2014-12-11, 19: 4 | 2014-12-11, 19:11
2014-12- 8, 21:30 | 2014-12- 8, 21:37      2014-12-10, 11:48 | 2014-12-10, 11:55      2014-12-11, 19:30 | 2014-12-11, 19:37
2014-12- 8, 21:52 | 2014-12- 8, 21:59      2014-12-10, 12:16 | 2014-12-10, 12:23      2014-12-11, 19:56 | 2014-12-11, 20: 4
2014-12- 8, 22:15 | 2014-12- 8, 22:22      2014-12-10, 12:45 | 2014-12-10, 12:52      2014-12-11, 20:23 | 2014-12-11, 20:30
2014-12- 8, 22:37 | 2014-12- 8, 22:44      2014-12-10, 13:14 | 2014-12-10, 13:21      2014-12-11, 20:49 | 2014-12-11, 20:57
2014-12- 8, 22:59 | 2014-12- 8, 23: 6      2014-12-10, 13:42 | 2014-12-10, 13:50      2014-12-11, 21:13 | 2014-12-11, 21:21
2014-12- 8, 23:22 | 2014-12- 8, 23:29      2014-12-10, 14:11 | 2014-12-10, 14:19      2014-12-11, 21:37 | 2014-12-11, 21:44
2014-12- 8, 23:44 | 2014-12- 8, 23:52      2014-12-10, 14:40 | 2014-12-10, 14:48      2014-12-11, 22: 1 | 2014-12-11, 22: 9
2014-12- 9, 0: 7 | 2014-12- 9, 0:14        2014-12-10, 15: 9 | 2014-12-10, 15:16      2014-12-11, 22:26 | 2014-12-11, 22:33
2014-12- 9, 0:30 | 2014-12- 9, 0:37        2014-12-10, 15:38 | 2014-12-10, 15:45      2014-12-11, 22:50 | 2014-12-11, 22:58
2014-12- 9, 0:53 | 2014-12- 9, 1: 0        2014-12-10, 16: 7 | 2014-12-10, 16:14      2014-12-11, 23:15 | 2014-12-11, 23:23
2014-12- 9, 1:16 | 2014-12- 9, 1:23        2014-12-10, 16:36 | 2014-12-10, 16:43      2014-12-11, 23:41 | 2014-12-11, 23:48
2014-12- 9, 1:39 | 2014-12- 9, 1:46        2014-12-10, 17: 5 | 2014-12-10, 17:12      2014-12-12, 0: 7 | 2014-12-12, 0:14
2014-12- 9, 2: 2 | 2014-12- 9, 2: 9        2014-12-10, 17:34 | 2014-12-10, 17:41      2014-12-12, 0:32 | 2014-12-12, 0:39
2014-12- 9, 2:25 | 2014-12- 9, 2:32        2014-12-10, 18: 3 | 2014-12-10, 18:10      2014-12-12, 0:58 | 2014-12-12, 1: 5
2014-12- 9, 2:48 | 2014-12- 9, 2:55        2014-12-10, 18:32 | 2014-12-10, 18:39      2014-12-12, 1:24 | 2014-12-12, 1:31
2014-12- 9, 3:11 | 2014-12- 9, 3:18        2014-12-10, 19: 1 | 2014-12-10, 19: 8      2014-12-12, 1:50 | 2014-12-12, 1:57
2014-12- 9, 3:35 | 2014-12- 9, 3:42        2014-12-10, 19:29 | 2014-12-10, 19:37      2014-12-12, 2:16 | 2014-12-12, 2:23
2014-12- 9, 3:58 | 2014-12- 9, 4: 5        2014-12-10, 19:58 | 2014-12-10, 20: 5      2014-12-12, 2:42 | 2014-12-12, 2:49
2014-12- 9, 4:22 | 2014-12- 9, 4:29        2014-12-10, 20:27 | 2014-12-10, 20:34      2014-12-12, 3: 8 | 2014-12-12, 3:15
2014-12- 9, 4:46 | 2014-12- 9, 4:53        2014-12-10, 20:55 | 2014-12-10, 21: 3      2014-12-12, 3:35 | 2014-12-12, 3:42
2014-12- 9, 5:10 | 2014-12- 9, 5:17        2014-12-10, 21:24 | 2014-12-10, 21:32      2014-12-12, 4: 1 | 2014-12-12, 4: 8
2014-12- 9, 5:35 | 2014-12- 9, 5:42        2014-12-10, 21:53 | 2014-12-10, 22: 0      2014-12-12, 4:27 | 2014-12-12, 4:34
2014-12- 9, 5:58 | 2014-12- 9, 6: 4        2014-12-10, 22:22 | 2014-12-10, 22:29      2014-12-12, 4:53 | 2014-12-12, 5: 0
2014-12- 9, 6:21 | 2014-12- 9, 6:28        2014-12-10, 22:50 | 2014-12-10, 22:58      2014-12-12, 5:20 | 2014-12-12, 5:27
2014-12- 9, 6:45 | 2014-12- 9, 6:52        2014-12-10, 23:19 | 2014-12-10, 23:27      2014-12-12, 5:47 | 2014-12-12, 5:54
2014-12- 9, 7:10 | 2014-12- 9, 7:17        2014-12-10, 23:48 | 2014-12-10, 23:55      2014-12-12, 6:13 | 2014-12-12, 6:20
2014-12- 9, 7:35 | 2014-12- 9, 7:42        2014-12-11, 0:17 | 2014-12-11, 0:24        2014-12-12, 6:40 | 2014-12-12, 6:47
2014-12- 9, 8: 0 | 2014-12- 9, 8: 7        2014-12-11, 0:46 | 2014-12-11, 0:53        2014-12-12, 7: 7 | 2014-12-12, 7:14
2014-12- 9, 8:26 | 2014-12- 9, 8:33        2014-12-11, 1:15 | 2014-12-11, 1:22        2014-12-12, 7:34 | 2014-12-12, 7:41
2014-12- 9, 8:52 | 2014-12- 9, 9: 0        2014-12-11, 1:43 | 2014-12-11, 1:51        2014-12-12, 8: 1 | 2014-12-12, 8: 8
2014-12- 9, 9:19 | 2014-12- 9, 9:26        2014-12-11, 2:12 | 2014-12-11, 2:20        2014-12-12, 8:28 | 2014-12-12, 8:35
2014-12- 9, 9:46 | 2014-12- 9, 9:53        2014-12-11, 2:42 | 2014-12-11, 2:49        2014-12-12, 8:55 | 2014-12-12, 9: 2
2014-12- 9, 10:13 | 2014-12- 9, 10:20      2014-12-11, 3:11 | 2014-12-11, 3:18        2014-12-12, 9:22 | 2014-12-12, 9:29
2014-12- 9, 10:39 | 2014-12- 9, 10:47      2014-12-11, 3:40 | 2014-12-11, 3:47        2014-12-12, 9:49 | 2014-12-12, 9:57
2014-12- 9, 11: 7 | 2014-12- 9, 11:14      2014-12-11, 4: 9 | 2014-12-11, 4:16        2014-12-12, 10:17 | 2014-12-12, 10:24
2014-12- 9, 11:34 | 2014-12- 9, 11:41      2014-12-11, 4:38 | 2014-12-11, 4:46        2014-12-12, 10:44 | 2014-12-12, 10:51
2014-12- 9, 12: 1 | 2014-12- 9, 12: 8      2014-12-11, 5: 7 | 2014-12-11, 5:15        2014-12-12, 11:11 | 2014-12-12, 11:18
2014-12- 9, 12:29 | 2014-12- 9, 12:36      2014-12-11, 5:36 | 2014-12-11, 5:44        2014-12-12, 11:39 | 2014-12-12, 11:46
2014-12- 9, 12:56 | 2014-12- 9, 13: 3      2014-12-11, 6: 5 | 2014-12-11, 6:13        2014-12-12, 12: 6 | 2014-12-12, 12:14
2014-12- 9, 13:24 | 2014-12- 9, 13:31      2014-12-11, 6:35 | 2014-12-11, 6:43        2014-12-12, 12:34 | 2014-12-12, 12:42
2014-12- 9, 13:52 | 2014-12- 9, 14: 0      2014-12-11, 7: 5 | 2014-12-11, 7:12        2014-12-12, 13: 2 | 2014-12-12, 13: 9
2014-12- 9, 14:21 | 2014-12- 9, 14:28      2014-12-11, 7:34 | 2014-12-11, 7:41        2014-12-12, 13:29 | 2014-12-12, 13:37
2014-12- 9, 14:49 | 2014-12- 9, 14:56      2014-12-11, 8: 3 | 2014-12-11, 8:10        2014-12-12, 13:57 | 2014-12-12, 14: 5
2014-12- 9, 15:18 | 2014-12- 9, 15:25      2014-12-11, 8:32 | 2014-12-11, 8:39        2014-12-12, 14:26 | 2014-12-12, 14:33
2014-12- 9, 15:46 | 2014-12- 9, 15:53      2014-12-11, 9: 1 | 2014-12-11, 9: 8        2014-12-12, 14:53 | 2014-12-12, 15: 1
2014-12- 9, 16:14 | 2014-12- 9, 16:21      2014-12-11, 9:30 | 2014-12-11, 9:38        2014-12-12, 15:21 | 2014-12-12, 15:28
2014-12- 9, 16:43 | 2014-12- 9, 16:50      2014-12-11, 9:59 | 2014-12-11, 10: 7       2014-12-12, 15:48 | 2014-12-12, 15:56
2014-12- 9, 17:11 | 2014-12- 9, 17:18      2014-12-11, 10:28 | 2014-12-11, 10:36      2014-12-12, 16:16 | 2014-12-12, 16:24
2014-12- 9, 17:39 | 2014-12- 9, 17:46      2014-12-11, 10:57 | 2014-12-11, 11: 5      2014-12-12, 16:44 | 2014-12-12, 16:52
2014-12- 9, 18: 8 | 2014-12- 9, 18:15      2014-12-11, 11:26 | 2014-12-11, 11:34      2014-12-12, 17:12 | 2014-12-12, 17:19
2014-12- 9, 18:36 | 2014-12- 9, 18:43      2014-12-11, 11:56 | 2014-12-11, 12: 4      2014-12-12, 17:40 | 2014-12-12, 17:47
2014-12- 9, 19: 5 | 2014-12- 9, 19:12      2014-12-11, 12:26 | 2014-12-11, 12:33      2014-12-12, 18: 7 | 2014-12-12, 18:15
2014-12- 9, 19:34 | 2014-12- 9, 19:41      2014-12-11, 12:55 | 2014-12-11, 13: 2      2014-12-12, 18:35 | 2014-12-12, 18:43
2014-12- 9, 20: 3 | 2014-12- 9, 20:10      2014-12-11, 13:18 | 2014-12-11, 13:27      2014-12-12, 19: 4 | 2014-12-12, 19:11
2014-12- 9, 20:32 | 2014-12- 9, 20:39      2014-12-11, 13:40 | 2014-12-11, 13:48      2014-12-12, 19:32 | 2014-12-12, 19:40
```

2014-12-12, 20: 1 | 2014-12-12, 20: 8
2014-12-12, 20:29 | 2014-12-12, 20:36
2014-12-12, 20:57 | 2014-12-12, 21: 4
2014-12-12, 21:25 | 2014-12-12, 21:32
2014-12-12, 21:53 | 2014-12-12, 22: 1
2014-12-12, 22:22 | 2014-12-12, 22:29
2014-12-12, 22:50 | 2014-12-12, 22:58
2014-12-12, 23:18 | 2014-12-12, 23:25
2014-12-12, 23:46 | 2014-12-12, 23:54
2014-12-13, 0:15 | 2014-12-13, 0:22
2014-12-13, 0:43 | 2014-12-13, 0:50
2014-12-13, 1:11 | 2014-12-13, 1:19
2014-12-13, 1:40 | 2014-12-13, 1:47
2014-12-13, 2: 8 | 2014-12-13, 2:15
2014-12-13, 2:36 | 2014-12-13, 2:44
2014-12-13, 3: 5 | 2014-12-13, 3:12
2014-12-13, 3:33 | 2014-12-13, 3:41
2014-12-13, 4: 2 | 2014-12-13, 4: 9
2014-12-13, 4:30 | 2014-12-13, 4:38
2014-12-13, 4:59 | 2014-12-13, 5: 6
2014-12-13, 5:27 | 2014-12-13, 5:34
2014-12-13, 5:55 | 2014-12-13, 6: 3
2014-12-13, 6:24 | 2014-12-13, 6:31
2014-12-13, 6:52 | 2014-12-13, 7: 0
2014-12-13, 7:21 | 2014-12-13, 7:29
2014-12-13, 7:50 | 2014-12-13, 7:57
2014-12-13, 8:18 | 2014-12-13, 8:26
2014-12-13, 8:47 | 2014-12-13, 8:54
2014-12-13, 9:15 | 2014-12-13, 9:23
2014-12-13, 9:44 | 2014-12-13, 9:51
2014-12-13, 10:12 | 2014-12-13, 10:20
2014-12-13, 10:41 | 2014-12-13, 10:49
2014-12-13, 11:10 | 2014-12-13, 11:17
2014-12-13, 11:39 | 2014-12-13, 11:46
2014-12-13, 12: 7 | 2014-12-13, 12:14
2014-12-13, 12:36 | 2014-12-13, 12:44
2014-12-13, 13: 5 | 2014-12-13, 13:13
2014-12-13, 13:34 | 2014-12-13, 13:42
2014-12-13, 14: 4 | 2014-12-13, 14:12
2014-12-13, 14:34 | 2014-12-13, 14:42
2014-12-13, 15: 3 | 2014-12-13, 15:11
2014-12-13, 15:33 | 2014-12-13, 15:40
2014-12-13, 16: 2 | 2014-12-13, 16: 9
2014-12-13, 16:31 | 2014-12-13, 16:39
2014-12-13, 17: 0 | 2014-12-13, 17: 8
2014-12-13, 17:29 | 2014-12-13, 17:37
2014-12-13, 17:58 | 2014-12-13, 18: 5
2014-12-13, 18:26 | 2014-12-13, 18:34
2014-12-13, 18:56 | 2014-12-13, 19: 3
2014-12-13, 19:24 | 2014-12-13, 19:32
2014-12-13, 19:53 | 2014-12-13, 20: 0
2014-12-13, 20:21 | 2014-12-13, 20:29
2014-12-13, 20:50 | 2014-12-13, 20:57
2014-12-13, 21:18 | 2014-12-13, 21:26
2014-12-13, 21:47 | 2014-12-13, 21:55
2014-12-13, 22:16 | 2014-12-13, 22:23
2014-12-13, 22:44 | 2014-12-13, 22:52
2014-12-13, 23:13 | 2014-12-13, 23:20
2014-12-13, 23:41 | 2014-12-13, 23:49
2014-12-14, 0:10 | 2014-12-14, 0:17
2014-12-14, 0:38 | 2014-12-14, 0:46
2014-12-14, 1: 7 | 2014-12-14, 1:15
2014-12-14, 1:36 | 2014-12-14, 1:43
2014-12-14, 2: 4 | 2014-12-14, 2:12
2014-12-14, 2:33 | 2014-12-14, 2:40
2014-12-14, 3: 1 | 2014-12-14, 3: 9
2014-12-14, 3:30 | 2014-12-14, 3:37
2014-12-14, 3:59 | 2014-12-14, 4: 6

2014-12-14, 4:27 | 2014-12-14, 4:35
2014-12-14, 4:56 | 2014-12-14, 5: 3
2014-12-14, 5:25 | 2014-12-14, 5:32
2014-12-14, 5:53 | 2014-12-14, 6: 0
2014-12-14, 6:21 | 2014-12-14, 6:28
2014-12-14, 6:49 | 2014-12-14, 6:57
2014-12-14, 7:18 | 2014-12-14, 7:25
2014-12-14, 7:46 | 2014-12-14, 7:53
2014-12-14, 8:14 | 2014-12-14, 8:22
2014-12-14, 8:43 | 2014-12-14, 8:50
2014-12-14, 9:11 | 2014-12-14, 9:18
2014-12-14, 9:38 | 2014-12-14, 9:46
2014-12-14, 10: 4 | 2014-12-14, 10:11
2014-12-14, 10:31 | 2014-12-14, 10:38
2014-12-14, 10:58 | 2014-12-14, 11: 5
2014-12-14, 11:25 | 2014-12-14, 11:33
2014-12-14, 11:53 | 2014-12-14, 12: 1
2014-12-14, 12:21 | 2014-12-14, 12:29
2014-12-14, 12:49 | 2014-12-14, 12:56
2014-12-14, 13:17 | 2014-12-14, 13:24
2014-12-14, 13:45 | 2014-12-14, 13:52
2014-12-14, 14:10 | 2014-12-14, 14:18
2014-12-14, 14:36 | 2014-12-14, 14:43
2014-12-14, 15: 3 | 2014-12-14, 15:10
2014-12-14, 15:30 | 2014-12-14, 15:37
2014-12-14, 15:58 | 2014-12-14, 16: 5
2014-12-14, 16:26 | 2014-12-14, 16:33
2014-12-14, 16:54 | 2014-12-14, 17: 1
2014-12-14, 17:21 | 2014-12-14, 17:29
2014-12-14, 17:49 | 2014-12-14, 17:57
2014-12-14, 18:18 | 2014-12-14, 18:25
2014-12-14, 18:46 | 2014-12-14, 18:53
2014-12-14, 19:14 | 2014-12-14, 19:21
2014-12-14, 19:42 | 2014-12-14, 19:49
2014-12-14, 20:10 | 2014-12-14, 20:18
2014-12-14, 20:39 | 2014-12-14, 20:47
2014-12-14, 21: 8 | 2014-12-14, 21:15
2014-12-14, 21:36 | 2014-12-14, 21:43
2014-12-14, 22: 4 | 2014-12-14, 22:11
2014-12-14, 22:32 | 2014-12-14, 22:40
2014-12-14, 23: 0 | 2014-12-14, 23: 8
2014-12-14, 23:28 | 2014-12-14, 23:36
2014-12-14, 23:57 | 2014-12-15, 0: 4
2014-12-15, 0:25 | 2014-12-15, 0:33
2014-12-15, 0:54 | 2014-12-15, 1: 1
2014-12-15, 1:22 | 2014-12-15, 1:29
2014-12-15, 1:50 | 2014-12-15, 1:57
2014-12-15, 2:18 | 2014-12-15, 2:26
2014-12-15, 2:46 | 2014-12-15, 2:54
2014-12-15, 3:15 | 2014-12-15, 3:22
2014-12-15, 3:43 | 2014-12-15, 3:51
2014-12-15, 4:11 | 2014-12-15, 4:19
2014-12-15, 4:40 | 2014-12-15, 4:47
2014-12-15, 5: 8 | 2014-12-15, 5:15
2014-12-15, 5:36 | 2014-12-15, 5:43
2014-12-15, 6: 4 | 2014-12-15, 6:11
2014-12-15, 6:32 | 2014-12-15, 6:40
2014-12-15, 7: 0 | 2014-12-15, 7: 8
2014-12-15, 7:29 | 2014-12-15, 7:36
2014-12-15, 7:57 | 2014-12-15, 8: 4
2014-12-15, 8:25 | 2014-12-15, 8:33
2014-12-15, 8:54 | 2014-12-15, 9: 1
2014-12-15, 9:22 | 2014-12-15, 9:30
2014-12-15, 9:51 | 2014-12-15, 9:58
2014-12-15, 10:19 | 2014-12-15, 10:27
2014-12-15, 10:48 | 2014-12-15, 10:56
2014-12-15, 11:16 | 2014-12-15, 11:24
2014-12-15, 11:45 | 2014-12-15, 11:53

2014-12-15, 12:14 | 2014-12-15, 12:21
2014-12-15, 12:42 | 2014-12-15, 12:50
2014-12-15, 13:11 | 2014-12-15, 13:18
2014-12-15, 13:39 | 2014-12-15, 13:46
2014-12-15, 14: 7 | 2014-12-15, 14:14
2014-12-15, 14:35 | 2014-12-15, 14:42
2014-12-15, 15: 3 | 2014-12-15, 15:10
2014-12-15, 15:30 | 2014-12-15, 15:38
2014-12-15, 15:58 | 2014-12-15, 16: 6
2014-12-15, 16:27 | 2014-12-15, 16:34
2014-12-15, 16:55 | 2014-12-15, 17: 2
2014-12-15, 17:22 | 2014-12-15, 17:30
2014-12-15, 17:50 | 2014-12-15, 17:58
2014-12-15, 18:18 | 2014-12-15, 18:26
2014-12-15, 18:46 | 2014-12-15, 18:54
2014-12-15, 19:14 | 2014-12-15, 19:22
2014-12-15, 19:42 | 2014-12-15, 19:50
2014-12-15, 20:10 | 2014-12-15, 20:18
2014-12-15, 20:38 | 2014-12-15, 20:46
2014-12-15, 21: 6 | 2014-12-15, 21:13
2014-12-15, 21:33 | 2014-12-15, 21:41
2014-12-15, 22: 1 | 2014-12-15, 22: 9
2014-12-15, 22:29 | 2014-12-15, 22:37
2014-12-15, 22:57 | 2014-12-15, 23: 5
2014-12-15, 23:25 | 2014-12-15, 23:33
2014-12-15, 23:53 | 2014-12-16, 0: 1
2014-12-16, 0:21 | 2014-12-16, 0:29
2014-12-16, 0:49 | 2014-12-16, 0:57
2014-12-16, 1:17 | 2014-12-16, 1:25
2014-12-16, 1:45 | 2014-12-16, 1:53
2014-12-16, 2:14 | 2014-12-16, 2:21
2014-12-16, 2:42 | 2014-12-16, 2:50
2014-12-16, 3:10 | 2014-12-16, 3:18
2014-12-16, 3:38 | 2014-12-16, 3:45
2014-12-16, 4: 5 | 2014-12-16, 4:13
2014-12-16, 4:33 | 2014-12-16, 4:41
2014-12-16, 5: 2 | 2014-12-16, 5: 9
2014-12-16, 5:29 | 2014-12-16, 5:37
2014-12-16, 5:57 | 2014-12-16, 6: 5
2014-12-16, 6:25 | 2014-12-16, 6:32
2014-12-16, 6:53 | 2014-12-16, 7: 0
2014-12-16, 7:21 | 2014-12-16, 7:28
2014-12-16, 7:49 | 2014-12-16, 7:56
2014-12-16, 8:17 | 2014-12-16, 8:24
2014-12-16, 8:44 | 2014-12-16, 8:52
2014-12-16, 9:12 | 2014-12-16, 9:20
2014-12-16, 9:40 | 2014-12-16, 9:48
2014-12-16, 10: 8 | 2014-12-16, 10:16
2014-12-16, 10:36 | 2014-12-16, 10:44
2014-12-16, 11: 4 | 2014-12-16, 11:12
2014-12-16, 11:32 | 2014-12-16, 11:40
2014-12-16, 12: 0 | 2014-12-16, 12: 7
2014-12-16, 12:28 | 2014-12-16, 12:36
2014-12-16, 12:56 | 2014-12-16, 13: 4
2014-12-16, 13:25 | 2014-12-16, 13:33
2014-12-16, 13:54 | 2014-12-16, 14: 1
2014-12-16, 14:22 | 2014-12-16, 14:29
2014-12-16, 14:50 | 2014-12-16, 14:58
2014-12-16, 15:18 | 2014-12-16, 15:26
2014-12-16, 15:47 | 2014-12-16, 15:54
2014-12-16, 16:15 | 2014-12-16, 16:23
2014-12-16, 16:44 | 2014-12-16, 16:51
2014-12-16, 17:12 | 2014-12-16, 17:19
2014-12-16, 17:40 | 2014-12-16, 17:48
2014-12-16, 18: 8 | 2014-12-16, 18:16
2014-12-16, 18:36 | 2014-12-16, 18:44
2014-12-16, 19: 4 | 2014-12-16, 19:12
2014-12-16, 19:31 | 2014-12-16, 19:40

2014-12-16, 19:56 | 2014-12-16, 20: 4
2014-12-16, 20:19 | 2014-12-16, 20:26
2014-12-16, 20:44 | 2014-12-16, 20:51
2014-12-16, 21:10 | 2014-12-16, 21:18
2014-12-16, 21:37 | 2014-12-16, 21:45
2014-12-16, 22: 4 | 2014-12-16, 22:12
2014-12-16, 22:31 | 2014-12-16, 22:39
2014-12-16, 22:59 | 2014-12-16, 23: 7
2014-12-16, 23:27 | 2014-12-16, 23:34
2014-12-16, 23:55 | 2014-12-17, 0: 2
2014-12-17, 0:22 | 2014-12-17, 0:30
2014-12-17, 0:50 | 2014-12-17, 0:58
2014-12-17, 1:18 | 2014-12-17, 1:26
2014-12-17, 1:46 | 2014-12-17, 1:54
2014-12-17, 2:14 | 2014-12-17, 2:22
2014-12-17, 2:42 | 2014-12-17, 2:50
2014-12-17, 3:10 | 2014-12-17, 3:18
2014-12-17, 3:38 | 2014-12-17, 3:46
2014-12-17, 4: 7 | 2014-12-17, 4:15
2014-12-17, 4:35 | 2014-12-17, 4:42
2014-12-17, 5: 3 | 2014-12-17, 5:11
2014-12-17, 5:31 | 2014-12-17, 5:39
2014-12-17, 5:59 | 2014-12-17, 6: 7
2014-12-17, 6:27 | 2014-12-17, 6:35
2014-12-17, 6:55 | 2014-12-17, 7: 3
2014-12-17, 7:23 | 2014-12-17, 7:30
2014-12-17, 7:51 | 2014-12-17, 7:58
2014-12-17, 8:19 | 2014-12-17, 8:26
2014-12-17, 8:47 | 2014-12-17, 8:54
2014-12-17, 9:15 | 2014-12-17, 9:23
2014-12-17, 9:43 | 2014-12-17, 9:51
2014-12-17, 10:11 | 2014-12-17, 10:19
2014-12-17, 10:39 | 2014-12-17, 10:46
2014-12-17, 11: 7 | 2014-12-17, 11:14
2014-12-17, 11:35 | 2014-12-17, 11:42
2014-12-17, 12: 3 | 2014-12-17, 12:10
2014-12-17, 12:31 | 2014-12-17, 12:38
2014-12-17, 12:58 | 2014-12-17, 13: 6
2014-12-17, 13:26 | 2014-12-17, 13:33
2014-12-17, 13:54 | 2014-12-17, 14: 1
2014-12-17, 14:22 | 2014-12-17, 14:29
2014-12-17, 14:50 | 2014-12-17, 14:57
2014-12-17, 15:18 | 2014-12-17, 15:25
2014-12-17, 15:46 | 2014-12-17, 15:53
2014-12-17, 16:14 | 2014-12-17, 16:21
2014-12-17, 16:42 | 2014-12-17, 16:50
2014-12-17, 17:10 | 2014-12-17, 17:18
2014-12-17, 17:38 | 2014-12-17, 17:46
2014-12-17, 18: 7 | 2014-12-17, 18:14
2014-12-17, 18:35 | 2014-12-17, 18:42
2014-12-17, 19: 0 | 2014-12-17, 19: 9
2014-12-17, 19:25 | 2014-12-17, 19:32
2014-12-17, 19:50 | 2014-12-17, 19:57
2014-12-17, 20:15 | 2014-12-17, 20:23
2014-12-17, 20:41 | 2014-12-17, 20:48
2014-12-17, 21: 7 | 2014-12-17, 21:14
2014-12-17, 21:32 | 2014-12-17, 21:40
2014-12-17, 21:58 | 2014-12-17, 22: 6
2014-12-17, 22:24 | 2014-12-17, 22:32
2014-12-17, 22:50 | 2014-12-17, 22:58
2014-12-17, 23:16 | 2014-12-17, 23:24
2014-12-17, 23:43 | 2014-12-17, 23:50
2014-12-18, 0: 9 | 2014-12-18, 0:16
2014-12-18, 0:35 | 2014-12-18, 0:42
2014-12-18, 1: 1 | 2014-12-18, 1: 8
2014-12-18, 1:27 | 2014-12-18, 1:35
2014-12-18, 1:54 | 2014-12-18, 2: 1
2014-12-18, 2:21 | 2014-12-18, 2:28
2014-12-18, 2:47 | 2014-12-18, 2:54
2014-12-18, 3:14 | 2014-12-18, 3:21
2014-12-18, 3:41 | 2014-12-18, 3:48
2014-12-18, 4: 7 | 2014-12-18, 4:15
2014-12-18, 4:34 | 2014-12-18, 4:42
2014-12-18, 5: 2 | 2014-12-18, 5: 9
2014-12-18, 5:29 | 2014-12-18, 5:37
2014-12-18, 5:56 | 2014-12-18, 6: 4
2014-12-18, 6:24 | 2014-12-18, 6:32
2014-12-18, 6:52 | 2014-12-18, 6:59
2014-12-18, 7:20 | 2014-12-18, 7:27
2014-12-18, 7:47 | 2014-12-18, 7:56
2014-12-18, 8:13 | 2014-12-18, 8:20
2014-12-18, 8:39 | 2014-12-18, 8:47
2014-12-18, 9: 7 | 2014-12-18, 9:14
2014-12-18, 9:34 | 2014-12-18, 9:41
2014-12-18, 10: 1 | 2014-12-18, 10: 9
2014-12-18, 10:29 | 2014-12-18, 10:37
2014-12-18, 10:57 | 2014-12-18, 11: 5
2014-12-18, 11:25 | 2014-12-18, 11:33
2014-12-18, 11:53 | 2014-12-18, 12: 1
2014-12-18, 12:21 | 2014-12-18, 12:29
2014-12-18, 12:49 | 2014-12-18, 12:56
2014-12-18, 13:17 | 2014-12-18, 13:24
2014-12-18, 13:45 | 2014-12-18, 13:52
2014-12-18, 14:12 | 2014-12-18, 14:20
2014-12-18, 14:41 | 2014-12-18, 14:48
2014-12-18, 15: 4 | 2014-12-18, 15:12
2014-12-18, 15:28 | 2014-12-18, 15:35
2014-12-18, 15:51 | 2014-12-18, 15:59
2014-12-18, 16:15 | 2014-12-18, 16:22
2014-12-18, 16:39 | 2014-12-18, 16:46
2014-12-18, 17: 3 | 2014-12-18, 17:11
2014-12-18, 17:27 | 2014-12-18, 17:35
2014-12-18, 17:53 | 2014-12-18, 18: 0
2014-12-18, 18:19 | 2014-12-18, 18:26
2014-12-18, 18:45 | 2014-12-18, 18:53
2014-12-18, 19:12 | 2014-12-18, 19:19
2014-12-18, 19:39 | 2014-12-18, 19:46
2014-12-18, 20: 6 | 2014-12-18, 20:14
2014-12-18, 20:33 | 2014-12-18, 20:41
2014-12-18, 21: 0 | 2014-12-18, 21: 8
2014-12-18, 21:27 | 2014-12-18, 21:35
2014-12-18, 21:55 | 2014-12-18, 22: 2
2014-12-18, 22:22 | 2014-12-18, 22:29
2014-12-18, 22:49 | 2014-12-18, 22:57
2014-12-18, 23:17 | 2014-12-18, 23:24
2014-12-18, 23:44 | 2014-12-18, 23:51